THE COMMON SENSE 80%

The Absolute Political Majority

BY
KENT EMMONS

Foreword by Andrew Wilkow

"The only thing necessary for the triumph of evil is for good men to do nothing."

~ Edmund Burke

Dedication

—ɯ—

This book is dedicated to my parents, Sandy and Jack Emmons, and to my two amazing, free-market capitalist daughters, Ashley and Aubrey. My parents are two of the wisest people I know; they have been my inspiration, mentors and guides throughout life, business and politics for 50+ years. My father invested nearly thirty years in building and leading the largest community bank in rural southern Illinois. After Dad retired from banking, he continued to dedicate his life to public service by serving as finance commissioner on his city council for 16 years.

Even though Illinois is one of the most corrupt and cash-strapped states in America, Dad made sure that his city remained fiscally sound and well-managed under his leadership. His secret? He and his fellow councilmen governed their city responsibly on a local level, doing their best to keep the federal government out of the local and state governments.

As finance commissioner, he was wise enough to understand that managing things locally creates value for constituents, much more value than if managed from afar. The further away a tax dollar gets sent from home, the more that tax dollar is diluted by poorly run state and federal bureaucrats and the programs they "manage." Often, those programs end up costing the local people more by way of wasteful, unfunded mandates and regulations that are sent "from above" (D.C.). From the surface, they appear to be well-meaning regulations, but have we seen those programs and projects work out on a federal level?

NOPE!

Dad realized that a community could, does and should take care of its own. He encouraged the members of his community to thrive, build businesses, work hard and give back by serving the community. He made it a point to treat his constituents and banking customers with the same level of independence and respect that each person deserved. Whether they were rich, poor, young, old, black, white or purple, all were respected from the heart.

While my dad was a big inspiration for writing The Common Sense 80%, my mom, (as those in our little hometown will tell you), is the wizard behind the curtain. To those who don't know her, she may seem quiet and shy, but the truth is her brilliance, wit and influence remain ten steps ahead of the rest of us. She embodies personal responsibility. On the home-front, she made sure that the family and finances were always in order so Dad could work unfettered to serve his community and empower everyone with whom he came in contact.

As a young kid, I had a fiercely independent streak that landed me in the principal's office more times than I care to remember, and that streak followed me well into my 30s. I was totally out of control, engaged in a non-stop party that included a lot of "wine, women and song." Nevertheless, Mom and Dad never put me in a gunnysack and threw me in the Wabash River. For that, I credit them and hereby nominate them for well-deserved sainthood!

Fortunately, those days have long since passed and I, like many folks my age and younger, have sobered up to the reality that our country is going to hell in a handbasket quickly. As a result, we have decided that we are NOT going to idly stand by and watch it happen!

One of the many reasons this book, the 2016 election and the many "common sense" movements now gaining huge traction across the nation are so important to me is that I want my children and their children to have the same opportunities to start, grow and build a business and create wealth for themselves, just as the past five generations of the Emmons family have done. Both of my daughters (Ashley, 29, and Aubrey, 12) have amazing entrepreneurial streaks and have done VERY well in their respective fields. They also FULLY understand and have experienced how government over-regulation can stifle business.

Ash, with your spot-on real estate sales and investment prowess, and Aubrey, at only 12 years old, with your growing production company and equine enterprise in the belly of the bureaucratic beast that we jokingly refer to as "The Communist Republic of California," I am amazed and inspired by you both! Because of you two, I look forward to jumping out of bed every day just to see what you will do and create today. Your accomplishments are absolutely amazing, but it is because of your wonderfully deep and loving hearts and how you both give so much back to the community that I am as proud as any father could be. I love you both and am so excited for tomorrow!

True leadership and governing start with us, and it's time for us to take whatever steps are necessary to bring it back home.

We love our country, and we'll fight to get it back.

Will you join in?

"A much-needed real, raw and hard-hitting voice in a new era of politics! This is not the typical bitching and moaning of the usual political books that offer no solutions in the end. The Common Sense 80% approach is a fun read with an actual action plan that will work! Love it!"

— **Gary W. Goldstein, Producer**—*Pretty Woman, Under Siege*

"Kent has written a breezy, readable book. But it's not just a joyride. It's a 'common sense' call-to-action and a step-by-step handbook on what we must do to right our country NOW!"

—**Jim Jimirro**, Creator and founding CEO of The Disney Channel

"This is more than just a really funny guy writing about a serious topic! The Common Sense 80% is a modern-day manifesto that lays out a powerful, practical and doable method for actually draining the swamp and returning America back to the people. In this book, Kent takes a concept like 'Make America Great Again' and puts legs on it! And feet. And pants. And socks. And shoes."

—**Josh Feuerstein**, Social media personality

"As always, Kent is edgy, disruptive and right on point! Let the truth be told!"

—**Greg Reid**, Author, speaker and entrepreneur

"Emmons cuts to the heart of the big government crisis with recommendations which empower the people while ending the Washington, D.C. power monopoly. This important rethinking of the role of the federal government should be on everyone's must-read short list."

—**Rick Manning**, President of Americans for Limited Government

Table of Contents

—⁓—

Foreword

Kent Emmons is a "real deal" Hollywood entrepreneur. But unlike so many in the land of showbiz, he has chosen to step outside the plastic bubble. This book, The Common Sense 80%, The Absolute Political Majority, shares in part a title of the influential work of Thomas Paine's Common Sense, which many historians believe gave the average colonist reason to join the cause of the American Revolution. Emmons seeks here to reignite that spark of thought as it relates to today's modern, big government.

For generations, millions of Americans have been conditioned to believe that the government is made up of superior individuals whose job it is to "lord over the masses." Generation after generation has been led to believe that they should be thankful for the blessing and bounty provided to them by the guardians of Washington D.C. The truth, however, is the government has nothing to give that it first doesn't take from the citizenry. And what it takes it wastes masterfully, then demands more. The Constitution sets up not only a framework for government, but also the law that governs the government. Today we live with a government unrestrained. The citizen has been cornered into both a failing government-run education and retirement system, and we are only one step away from adding healthcare to the list.

Unlike many in the entertainment field who endlessly lavish praise on the governing class for "being here to help," while shielding their own money from being wasted, Kent decided to dive in and pen a book that would ask the right questions and provide the right answers. Readers will find themselves asking, "Why do we let them do that? Why do we pay for that? Why are they still there?" The Common Sense 80%, The Absolute Political Majority shows the reader where the government went astray of the Constitution and, more importantly, where it has failed to actually do the things it's supposed to do. The takeaway will be that this country cannot continue to elect the same type of people who linger for 25–30 years and think they are going to do anything differently. The very class of people who have become "Washington" promise to "change" or "fix" Washington every 2–4 years, only to make the mess they made bigger.

If you are done with platitudes and disposable promises... Read on.
—**Andrew Wilkow**, host of "The Wilkow Majority" on SiriusXM

Acknowledgements

—⚏—

There are hundreds of people who have made this book possible. First and absolutely foremost, "Uncle Doug" Crowe, the Book Master extraordinaire! Uncle Doug and I have literally worked on this book for several years, on five continents and had a total blast doing it! Uncle Doug and his international team have been the wheel-house for every draft and iteration of the pages that follow. I'm so thankful for his talent, perspective and, most importantly, our years and years of friendship!

Once the content and information for this book was compiled, it needed that magic touch and was placed into the hands of one of the most brilliant, vivacious, elegant, and big-thinking women I know, my dear friend Marites Rubio Cuevas. She is smart, witty and internationally politically astute (and as politically incorrect) as anyone I know! By having the ability to read my twisted mind, Marites brought it all together, wrapped it up and put a beautiful bow on it, and we laughed our asses off the entire way.

I also want to thank Andrew Wilkow for his wonderful foreword. The future of our country greatly depends on media outlets and personalities who have the balls to speak out, tell it like it is, call out who needs to be called out and just speak the truth. As Rush is to the older crowd, Andrew is to the younger crowd.

Introduction

—‹‹‹—

I'm not exactly sure when the tipping point occurred. But, in the last twenty years or so, two highly vocal and extreme minority groups took it upon themselves to be the spokespeople for all of us. On the right, claiming to be the final word on fiscal responsibility and moral purity, are the Republicans (a.k.a. conservatives). On the left, claiming to be the voice of the oppressed and downtrodden, are the Democrats (a.k.a. liberals). Both sides believe they represent approximately half of the American people. And both are wrong. Dead wrong.

When you study each party in its entirety, (i.e., what each "claims" to stand for), less than 20 percent of the population is fully on board with either side. Most people take only a handful of ideas or viewpoints from one side or the other, but are forced to affix a label to their beliefs. While over 80 percent of voting Americans align slightly closer with one side or the other, most would agree the actions on both sides are fundamentally wrong. The parties' approaches to government have taken America from what was once a relatively free country and transformed it into a bureaucratic cesspool. This gridlock of extremism is a rapidly growing cancer that is quickly killing the United States of America. Our country is wrought with debt and stifled by regulations that have made it almost impossible to do even the simplest things like getting a permit to improve your home or starting a business and giving yourself a shot at creating wealth, (unless you are one of the highly connected types like George Soros and Warren Buffett).

For recent generations, the extreme left or right has always drawn the attention on issues in the news. Because our common-sense position doesn't make for good sound bites, our voices are rarely heard—then came the last two election cycles.

This book is not about the extreme 10 percent fringe on the left or the 10 percent fringe on the right. This is about the 80 percent of us who wholeheartedly realize that a total governmental overhaul is needed. *Common Sense* 80% is a call to action for us: the formerly silent and unrepresented 80 percent of the American voters. We are the majority—the undisputed and overwhelming majority.

Most people, regardless of political affiliation, likely agree with most or all of the following statements:

- I care about citizens who are weak, old and/or poor and want them to have food and shelter.
- I value hard work and responsibility and believe that if you are able-bodied, you should earn your keep.
- I don't need the government to teach me morality.
- Establishment politicians are self-serving and don't have my best interests at heart.
- The federal government wastes money…a LOT of money.
- The federal government is highly inefficient.
- Until we can take care of our own citizens, we don't need to be bringing anyone else into the country unless they add value.
- The federal tax code and its enforcement is impossible to understand and needs to be overhauled and simplified.
- The federal government has four primary functions: military, monetary, judicial and postal. With a few exceptions, everything else can be managed more efficiently at the state and local levels.

I was raised in the rural Midwest in southern Illinois, where my parents taught me the value of hard work. They instilled in me that you help your community and yourself by empowering others to succeed. Commonly referred to as "flyover country" by my associates in New York and Los Angeles, Middle America is full of hardworking Midwesterners and is the heart and soul of our country. I also participate regularly in the world of finance, banking and entrepreneurship. This is at home in Tennessee, where risk, reward and hard work come together for those of us who are willing to take a gamble on creating value for ourselves and others and accepting responsibility for our actions.

The majority of folks living in New York and Los Angeles are clueless about the distinct cultural differences within our borders and the power that we "flyovers" wield. Until, that is, the reality of the 2016 election hit them square in the face. These two worlds of "city folks" and "flyover folks" could not be further apart. I am a "flyover folk" through-and-through, which means I could see the 2016 election coming from a mile away.

I am fortunate enough to live and work in two distinctly different worlds of entertainment and entrepreneurialism. My entertainment business takes me deep into the world of Hollywood. "Popular culture" has never defined the word *oxymoron* so precisely.

Celebrities, stars, musicians and artists draw massive amounts of media attention, especially those who aren't even truly respected. Like many celebrities nowadays, most establishment politicians are similarly held in low regard. If you're a celebrity or politician and you screw up today, you'll find your faux pas the lead joke on the latenight talk shows and the subject of demeaning YouTube videos. If you are fortunate, you may even host *Saturday Night Live* after you lose a campaign or upon the release of a tawdry sex video with someone you shouldn't be with. Either way, you're a star, baby! Hollywood loves a good laugh and the news loves a good fight.

It's like watching a train wreck. We know we shouldn't watch, but we can't pull ourselves away. Controversy gets ratings and ratings sell ad space.

The extreme opinions on the left and the right get airtime for the same reasons. Even today, the Common Sense 80% positions get very little press. We all pretty much agree on the same basic stuff! What is deemed as "newsworthy" is not necessarily relevant. The subjects of media debates don't apply to the day-to-day lives of most people. The issues and topics we discuss in this book and movement, however, personally affect each and every one of us, including our parents, children and grandchildren, regardless of political affiliation.

Those of us who would never fully pledge allegiance to either side have been essentially left without a political home. Until recently, with our two-party system, we were coerced to align ourselves as either a Democrat or a Republican. But, the majority of Americans are disgusted by both parties and the self-serving interests for which they stand. In 2016, when we peeked behind the curtains of both parties and learned how the system truly operates, we became ashamed to align ourselves with either group. A large percentage of voters cast their vote reluctantly for one party. It wasn't because they loved a particular candidate, but because they despised the contender on the other side.

Think about the primaries. By electing Donald Trump, Republican voters sent a nice big "F*** you!" to the Republican establishment, essentially telling the Bushes and Grahams where to get off. It was a total vote of no confidence for the Republican Party. On the Democratic side, Bernie Sanders had captured the hearts of a significant number of Democratic voters because they saw Hillary Clinton as part of the Democratic establishment. But when the DNC put "the fix" in for Hillary, voters saw they had no choice but to cast their votes for Clinton just because they were anti-Trump.

Since the 2016 presidential primaries, the majority of us are no longer Republicans or Democrats. We are the Common Sense 80%. We are

Americans who can and will do what we think is right. We pay our bills, raise our families and volunteer in our communities; all the while managing our personal and business affairs with integrity. It is because of this foundation of integrity and accountability that all of us are fed up with trillion-dollar deficits and irresponsible government. We make up about 80% of the registered voters in America. We are the Common Sense 80%.

We are the *absolute* majority.

Find a friend or coworker who you think is of a different political affiliation than you and start an intelligent conversation about the actual issues and direction this nation is taking. You'll discover you have more in common than you think. It's time to remove the labels of liberal and conservative, Democrat and Republican. While these extreme right- and left-wing idiots (also known as the "wingers") continue to rearrange the deck furniture on the *Titanic*, we, the Common Sense 80%, have mobilized. And we will see to it that the establishment gets a taste of their own unemployment medicine. We can offer up Common Sense 80% candidates for the House and Senate who are insulated from the corruption and cronyism that have infiltrated the foundation of our freedom. The Establishment, Politicians, Big Corporate Unions . . . these are just a few of the "wingers" that should no longer have a place to dominate policy.

Our fading memories of grade-school history class have damaged our ability to govern ourselves and instill passion in our purpose. Let me remind you in case you've forgotten. Our Founding Fathers were incredibly intelligent men. They experienced more injustice than today's U.S. citizens, but it seems we are getting closer and closer to the same pre-revolution-era tyranny. Our Founding Fathers saw the danger and the slippery slope that is abuse of power, much like we are seeing now. Therefore, they designed our federal government for 2 specific purposes: to protect the states' rights and protect and guarantee individual freedom for each and every one of us. The Constitution was designed to ensure fundamental freedom with the flexibility of amendments. The Bill of Rights covered all personal freedoms we now enjoy. These are the core reasons that we even have a federal government. Nowhere in any of these documents was there room for $1 million to improve "biking" signs or a $442,000 grant to study male prostitutes in Vietnam (yes, our government actually paid for them!).

I am a very positive person, but I am astounded by how many Americans think we, as a country, are "bulletproof." When our government lets the military erode, pushes their policies and regulations into areas of our life in which it has no business, and continually spends more dollars than it earns at an accelerated rate, the only outcome is national insolvency and the loss of personal freedom. Our generation has not experienced a full meltdown in this country—and those who would remind us, those who lived during the Great Depression of the 1930s, are becoming scarcer by the minute. We are the only ones responsible for ensuring that the freedoms we as Americans enjoy, the same freedoms that YOU and I are entitled to, the ones that have been the most sought-after in history, continue to exist. There are only 2 keys to safeguarding our freedoms: a fiscally sound economy and a strong national defense. Without either of these, we will collapse.

The looming national monetary crisis isn't fine wine, folks. It does not get better with age. It gets much worse. When you glance at the facts and graphs in this book, you may realize that debating issues like gay marriage doesn't seem as important as becoming financial slaves to countries like China. Even worse, we are held at the mercy of those crazy bastards in Saudi Arabia and Venezuela for oil, a resource of which we already have plenty within our own country. How likely are we to invest the bulk of our judicial resources in social issues when our brightest students are rated twenty-fifth or worse, behind nearly every developed country in the world? Our country is going to hell in a handbasket . . . quickly.

While fiscal irresponsibility is a significant driver of the mess our country is in, this book isn't merely about money. The policies, processes and entrenched cronyism in our governmental system have real life-and-death consequences for all Americans. Somehow, over the years, our "representatives" (and it's not just the members of Congress!) have taken on the role of dictating not only our personal healthcare but how we educate our kids in our local communities. They do this by way of self-serving the special interests of big corporations via their web of high-dollar lobbyists. Over time and without realizing it, we have resigned our freedom of choice to our federal lawmakers, letting them decide who we can marry or how to buckle a car seat. The bureaucrats are running the show now, leading the American people and Congress around by the nose. Those who used to be called our "public servants" have now mutated into a real version of the inmates running the asylum. And, they have the power to crush you with virtually no due process.

Our country has ventured down the road to fundamental and financial ruin. We have reached a point where an instant and dramatic reversal back to our core purpose is our only hope of maintaining the very freedom for which so many have sacrificed their reputations and lives. It's that serious.

As a country, we have enjoyed the most rapid rise to power in the history of the planet. Our abundance, wealth and prosperity were founded on "inalienable rights." Our freedom of speech, commerce and countless other forms of freedom have rarely been enjoyed by any other country in the history of the world. As stated in the best-selling book *How to Kill 11 Million People* by Andy Andrews, we have the longest running government in history. Other nations have been around longer than us; however, no one has had a democratic-republic government that has lasted this long.

Like many civilizations before us, prosperity and the freedom that help create it also come with responsibility. By letting Washington, D.C. creep into our homes, classrooms and businesses, we have delegated many of these personal responsibilities to the fox in the hen-house—the bureaucrats. The federal government, its agencies and the bureaucratic mentality that supports them have become a life-threatening tumor whose cells multiply every time a new bureaucrat is hired. The newbie "public servant," this innocent, well-meaning individual, quickly assimilates into a corrupt and irresponsible system, becoming a malignant social cancer cell who transforms into a member of a shameless "entitlement program" or department. In all but a few areas, local and state governments are much better suited to govern efficiently and effectively.

Regardless of your upbringing, liberals and conservatives alike will be hard-pressed to argue against the obvious bastardization of our foundation of freedom and the responsibility we must honor in order to keep it. We have traded one for the other, and unless action is taken swiftly and immediately, our country will continue to rapidly erode and fall the way that so many other former dominating superpowers have.

Inside these pages, you will find the unvarnished truth about what "our" government does, what it spends "our" money on, and what boondoggles its programs have morphed into, compared to how they started. You'll discover rather quickly that our current system of government and the freedom we are supposed to be enjoying are in peril. Like the Ottoman Empire, the Roman Empire and countless other fallen societies, we are destined to fall . . . and hard we will fall unless we take action now.

Taking action does not mean sitting around watching Fox News, CNN or MSNBC, or complaining at the water cooler. Action refers to *doing something*. The blueprint outlined in this book is the seed for swift, actionable and tangible change. Your involvement can and will make a difference!

Unlike many political and economic books, *The Common Sense 80%* comes with a one-page action plan and you can, as an empowered individual, take steps to execute this plan personally. Yes, you! This is your opportunity to contribute to the revolution that is happening and finally do something more than watch the talking heads on TV.

Having an intelligent discussion and taking action is easy when we take the Common Sense 80% approach. By steering our country back to the fundamentals of true leadership and personal responsibility, we can reverse the shameless and imploding path the United States is on. With this simple plan, we can return our country and our lives to the abundance and freedom that have been graciously handed to us by our Founding Fathers through blood, sweat and, in many instances, their very lives. Our Union has been a shining example of freedom through the creation and execution of the greatest document ever written—the U.S. Constitution.

We might be Democrats, Republicans, Independents, Libertarians or whatever way we define which "side" we're on. But at our core, we are Americans, and we are fed up with the entitled establishment. This action plan is certainly not for the establishment or die-hard Democrats or rank-and-file Republicans. They are the problem. Fortunately for us, those guys are now the minority, the "wingers." We, the Common Sense 80%, are the overwhelming majority, and we are taking charge. In fact, we now have an identity and a plan!

Read, share and take action. We have a once-in-a-lifetime chance to chart a new Common Sense 80% course and return our country to the fundamental freedom and abundance that we once earned and guarded as responsible Americans. We can still save our country. It is up to us to take action. NOW.

THE REVOLUTION IS ON!

Chapter One
What the Hell Happened?

—⚌—

"They who can give up essential liberty to obtain a little temporary safety deserve neither liberty nor safety."

—Benjamin Franklin

America is at a major crossroads.

For many years, you've heard the manufactured buzzwords in the news and at the water cooler—the bad economy, trillion-dollar deficits, healthcare, welfare, gay rights, government waste, tort reform, blah, blah, blah…How did we get here?

Over two hundred years ago, a few dozen bold and brilliant men, in order to form "a more perfect union," drafted some documents that shook the fabric of freedom for people on our planet. Dictators, kings and emperors ran countries prior to these documents. A grand social experiment began.

America broke away from England, and it was time to construct a new set of rules that would stand the test of time. The Founding Fathers spoke from the head and heart, and their words have shaped the freedoms that millions have given their very lives for.

They gave us a historic opportunity. True freedom was born.

Under the guidelines of our Constitution, our country flourished. The freedom afforded us under the Constitution was the catalyst that drove America to become the greatest super-power the world had ever seen. Because of that, we, as Americans, were granted the greatest privilege of all — PERSONAL FREEDOM.

Freedom to be educated, freedom to worship as we please and freedom to work hard, build and accumulate personal wealth. For a long time that's exactly what we did. Then at some point, while we were reveling in our abundance and distracted by destructive self-indulgence, the government slowly and quietly crept further and further into our lives, eventually turning us into slaves of an over-reaching bureaucracy that shows no sign of stopping. By becoming "rich," fat, lazy and disengaged, we have allowed a system corrupted by blood-sucking bureaucrats and big-dollar lobbyists to ruin it for us.

"WE THE PEOPLE of the United States, in Order to form a more perfect Union, establish Justice, insure domestic Tranquility, provide for the common defence, promote the general Welfare, and secure the Blessings of Liberty to ourselves and our Posterity, do ordain and establish this Constitution for the United States of America."

I encourage you to read those words again. Read these words aloud to your children and dissect the essence of what it means to you today. At the time these words were written, men had shed their blood and risked **everything** to be able to create something never seen before: a government *by* and *for* the people. It was historical.

England was treating the colonies unfairly, so our ancestral pioneers declared independence from England. They told England, "We're breaking up with you." Those who put their signatures on the Declaration of Independence were knowingly signing their own death warrants. The persecution of freedoms was so intolerable that they believed a free and *united* states had more value than their personal wealth, lands and even their very lives. It wasn't but a few years when the individual states realized that in order to "form a more perfect union," the colonies should form a new country. The framers of the Constitution recognized this document would need to stand the test of time.

The founders knew that there were very few functions that could be stronger as a cooperative than individually. Military, monetary, postal and judiciary—these systems were designed to handle constitutional issues ONLY. The federal government wasn't formed in order to hand down edicts that decide who can use which restrooms. Members of Congress, however, could draft amendments and, upon approval by a majority, the Constitution could grow with the changing landscape. While the founders couldn't predict the internet or someone's desire to rob the U.S. Treasury of $168,000 to study blue monkey feces in Africa (completely true), they did understand the document had to have a clear direction and fundamentals that were timeless. The fundamentals in this document were supposed to ensure that our freedom would be protected from outside and, even equally importantly, inside our borders. Washington, Franklin, Madison and other leaders experienced firsthand that the dangers from abroad were equal to the dangers of excessive, internal governmental power.

As the Constitution was framed, it was hotly debated. The debate over strong versus weak governmental powers (or centralization versus decentralization) was a highly contested and challenging aspect of building the new government. Northern politicians like Hamilton supported a very strong, centralized government, while the southern Jeffersonian contingent wanted a weaker federal government that would protect its people but allow the states to operate as independent entities. This debate arose in response to the new nation's desire to combat enemies within the country. (Do you see a pattern here?)

In the end, they all agreed that handing anyone too much power for too long meant certain tyranny equal to, or even worse than, that of the King of England.

"Power tends to corrupt, and absolute power corrupts absolutely."

—Sir John Dalberg-Acton

Even though the above words from English historian, author and politician Sir John Dalberg-Acton were crafted nearly one hundred years after the drafting of our Constitution, our Founding Fathers knew and understood them intuitively. Consider the eighteen points in Article 1, Section 8 of the Constitution where the specific role of the federal government is outlined clearly and succinctly:

Article 1, Section 8

1: The Congress shall have Power To lay and collect Taxes, Duties, Imposts and Excises, to pay the Debts and provide for the common Defence and general Welfare of the United States; but all Duties, Imposts and Excises shall be uniform throughout the United States;

2: To borrow Money on the credit of the United States;

3: To regulate Commerce with foreign Nations, and among the several States, and with the Indian Tribes;

4: To establish an uniform Rule of Naturalization, and uniform Laws on the subject of Bankruptcies throughout the United States;

5: To coin Money, regulate the Value thereof, and of foreign Coin, and fix the Standard of Weights and Measures;

6: To provide for the Punishment of counterfeiting the Securities and current Coin of the United States;

7: To establish Post Offices and post Roads;

8: To promote the Progress of Science and useful Arts, by securing for limited Times to Authors and Inventors the exclusive Right to their respective Writings and Discoveries;

9: To constitute Tribunals inferior to the supreme Court;

10: To define and punish Piracies and Felonies committed on the high Seas, and Offenses against the Law of Nations;

11: To declare War, grant Letters of Marque and Reprisal, and make Rules concerning Captures on Land and Water;

12: To raise and support Armies, but no Appropriation of Money to that Use shall be for a longer Term than two Years;

13: To provide and maintain a Navy;

14: To make Rules for the Government and Regulation of the land and naval Forces;

15: To provide for calling forth the Militia to execute the Laws of the Union, suppress Insurrections and repel Invasions;

16: To provide for organizing, arming, and disciplining, the Militia, and for governing such Part of them as may be employed in the Service of the United States, reserving to the States respectively, the Appointment of the Officers, and the Authority of training the Militia according to the discipline prescribed by Congress;

17: To exercise exclusive Legislation in all Cases whatsoever, over such District (not exceeding ten Miles square) as may, by Cession of particular States, and the Acceptance of Congress, become the Seat of the Government of the United States, and to exercise like Authority over all Places purchased by the Consent of the Legislature of the State in which the Same shall be, for the Erection of Forts, Magazines, Arsenals, dock-Yards and other needful Buildings;—And

18: To make all Laws which shall be necessary and proper for carrying into Execution the foregoing Powers, and all other Powers vested by this Constitution in the Government of the United States, or in any Department or Officer thereof.

Unfortunately, we have forgotten these timeless words and therefore these powers have been corrupted. (Note that there isn't any item there that allows for studying monkey feces. The framers couldn't see the value in it, even in 1787.) In the name of "helping others," the establishment and their bureaucratic minions have twisted, bent and distorted the very essence of the Constitution.

In fact, the Tenth Amendment states explicitly what the federal government's responsibility is *to the contrary:*

Amendment X

The powers not delegated to the United States by the Constitution, nor prohibited by it to the States, are reserved to the States respectively, or to the people.

According to the above, ANY issue not expressly addressed in the Constitution is exclusively at the will of the state. The vast majority of the current federal laws, programs, initiatives and departments were not supposed to be controlled at the federal level—EVER. These decisions are "reserved to the States respectively, or to the people." The states, counties and cities that govern responsibly will flourish, and those who govern irresponsibly will reap what they sow.

Abortion? Not allowed to be determined by the federal government. Seat belt laws? Nope.

Gay marriage? Not the federal government's domain. Education? Seriously?

Since the U.S. Department of Education was formed, students of our sacred republic have gone from being one of the world leaders in education in math and science to settling for an embarrassing national ranking of 30th in math and 19th in reading behind countries like Slovenia and Poland. Brilliant!

Take what Jefferson and his fellow leaders wrote, place it squarely against the "government" that we see today, and consider what has become of our country. You'll discover how far our once great country has unknowingly regressed. The power our generation has bestowed upon the federal government through ignorance and indifference has been corrupted . . . absolutely.

This is not liberal whining or Tea Party political ranting, nor is it alarmist rhetoric or political spin. The truth is irrefutable. What we choose to do with this truth is totally up to us. Look at the results of the last two election cycles! When a good, new candidate steps up and runs, the establishments from both parties are being shown the door. True Americans are fed up by the establishment.

For all practical purposes, the establishment, as we know it now, is finished. The era of the Bushes, Clintons and the like is over. It is now our time to step up and take charge with absolute conviction and NO compromise. We now have the power and the will of the people to affect change we know is necessary. We only require the courage of our convictions—yours and mine.

Our Founding Fathers knew firsthand how easily a government based on religion, hierarchical assembly and abusive power could enslave a population. Our Constitution was specifically designed to ensure against an oppressive, intrusive and corrupt government. Their "framework" was eloquently written on six pages....only SIX pages! Consider the historical meaning of this. The framers were all learned men. They had suffered serious oppression from England and decided to make an extremely bold, costly and decisive move toward freedom. Their number one objective was to make sure that a constitution for a new nation prevented any chance of perversion. They knew they were creating a society that would be the envy of the world.

I have been fortunate enough to have personally traveled to dozens of countries all over the world. Believe me — we are the envy of the world. But little do our foreign friends realize that the finances and foreign affairs of our beloved United States are in complete shambles. They have yet to discover the fact that the United States government, complete with its self-aggrandizing pomp and circumstance, is little more than a paper tiger. In fact, we are so close to economic enslavement to China and oil-rich counties such as Saudi Arabia that up until a tough leader like President Trump came along, they didn't see the U.S. as a threat in any way, shape or form. Just as smaller and weaker countries are seen as mere annoyances to us, my conversations with business leaders in China and advisors to the King of Saudi Arabia confirm the fact that we were rapidly gaining the reputation of an impotent country.

Shockingly, the general population of the world still believes the horseshit rhetoric that D.C. politicians and spin doctors continue to puke into their microphones and their loudspeakers. Can you imagine what the Founding Fathers would think if they were around today to see what the federal government has become? The Founders gave their blood, sweat, tears and lives . . . for what? So our career politicians can live the high life in the D.C. bubble while allowing our freedom to erode? I don't think so.

According to the National Archives, there are now 175,496 pages in the Code of Federal Regulations, which is 146% increase in the number of pages since 1975. The U.S. Chamber of Commerce calculated the cost of compliance for all federal regulations as $1.9 trillion annually, and 70% of those regulations are economical, costing $1.3 trillion. The annual cost of federal regulation and intervention in 2017 was an estimated $1.9 trillion, which was 20% higher than the average for all businesses. The report also noted environmental regulations cost $394 billion, tax compliance rules $316 billion, and occupational safety and health and homeland security cost $253 billion.

What does that mean for each of us personally? According to a 2015 study, each American household would be responsible for $15,586 of the federal regulatory burden. Further, as of 2015, small businesses faced an annual regulatory cost of $11,724 per employee.

We have allowed ourselves to slide into the enslavement of a faceless, bloated and irresponsible government by not paying attention to what is truly going on in Washington. We true Americans have locked ourselves in a prison of our own making. As children, we are told how "free" we are. But for decades, our federal government has been telling us they can do a better job of "providing freedom," making decisions and reinforcing "values" better than our local governments, communities or even our own families.

Our personal freedom is quickly eroding as the establishment in Washington shockingly gets more powerful and irresponsible. Without exception, every time a new government regulation is passed, we lose freedom.

Every. Single. Time.

We don't need to judge or rationalize the regulation. A regulation, by its very nature, is transferring our freedom to choose and empower the government to manage our life, our family and our destiny. The government, like Lindsay

Lohan, started out sweet, pure and kind. Over time, the various cadres of self-serving handlers sucked the life and the honor out of the persona. Just as poor Lindsay became irresponsible, unaccountable and totally out of control, our federal government no longer has honorable leadership, direction or fiscal sobriety. We— you and I—are the only chance our country has for a true "rehab." Let's take a look at some of the bureaucratic offenders that have been stripping us of our personal freedom. And let's form an action plan to take our freedoms back and send the bureaucrats packing once and for all.

As always, it begins with the money . . .

Chapter Two

First We Cut the Fat. A LOT of Fat.

—⚊—

"It is a popular delusion that the government wastes vast amounts of money through inefficiency and sloth. Enormous effort and elaborate planning are required to waste this much money."

—P.J. O'Rourke

What do you know about the federal government? Bloated, inefficient, poorly managed and wasting A LOT of money! Your money!

What if we could reduce the size of the federal government by over 80%, and the remaining 20% could be staffed by people who truly are public servants. Imagine our government running efficiently AND you never having to file a tax return again.

Are we dreaming?

The plan inside these pages gives the federal government the proverbial efficiency enema that it has sorely needed for years. It's not only possible but elegantly simple, provided we set aside our conventions and assumptions. It's an easy plan, but it will take a LOT of action on our part.

Implementing this plan will outrage politicians and bureaucrats who make a living off the way the federal government currently operates. They will call it "radical" and "crazy" and say it is impossible to achieve. They will fight it tooth and nail. They need the big, fat government system of today to continue to operate and grow as is so they can keep their fat-paying jobs. To them, it's the bigger the government, the better. Big government means more money and less accountability for the political class and bureaucrats. Our good friends at Turning Point USA said it best on their t-shirts, "BIG GOVERNMENT SUCKS." True and simple.

The average person like you and me, who have small businesses and jobs, find it easy to understand this plan because we have to be accountable for our actions, live within our means, and meet our commitments or face serious consequences. We get it.

We know that it will take a lot of throwing out the old guard and putting in the new guard to put our plan into action. It's a big task, but we can do it. Why? Because there are more of us than there are of them.

As Americans, we can run for office with a straightforward, cohesive agenda and whip our country back into shape one House and Senate seat at a time. If we are not inclined to run, we can recruit and/ or support candidates that would run on that cohesive platform: the Common Sense 80% platform.

Ready? Here we go!

For such an audacious plan to work, we start with a combination of us, as individuals, stepping up and being personally accountable for our actions and taking immediate steps that will return a significant part of the regulatory duties back to the states and municipalities where they can be efficiently managed. It can be done, but it is up to you and me to make it happen.

We'll get to the action plan in just a bit. Before we explore the details, though, let's cover the big picture first. To begin with, why do you think the federal government is as bloated and inefficient as it is? The answer to this question is simple: common sense.

The reason our federal government was formed in the first place, (i.e. the founding of our great country which led to the creation of the Constitution and

Bill of Rights), was to make all states (individual colonies) combine resources and become a united force and draw strength to declare its independence from England. Its primary purposes were to form a military to defend the country from unwanted intruders like England or anyone else who might try to lay claim to our great land, establish a monetary system, build a postal structure and put in place a judicial system to defend people's rights under the constitution.

Military, Monetary, Postal and Judicial.

That's it! No ups, no extras.

Over the years, however, the federal government has managed to work its way into all areas of our lives in which it has no business, through thousands of poorly-run, bureaucrat-ridden departments, agencies and programs.

The biggest problem with these department programs and agencies is that they are made up of people who have limited real-world management skills and, in most cases, utterly zero practical experience in the area in which they are supposed to serve. They are there to push paper and create more work so as to justify them being there. If you have ever been an employee of the federal government and/or a member of any government workers' union, you know I'm not exaggerating. All you have to do is look at the management and budget structure of these departments.

So how did the federal government end up so bloated and out of control and start reaching WAY outside of the areas of Military, Monetary, Postal and Judicial and start intruding into our personal and business lives? It was a combination of a few things. As you continue reading, keep this in mind:

Every time the government adds a new regulation, department, "government service" or agency, we lose a little of our freedom. Every time! No exceptions. Because with "service" comes additional regulation. ALWAYS!

"Follow the money..."

—Henry E. Peterson

As the country became established, politicians began seeing opportunities to raid the coffers for themselves and their supporters by way of pet projects under the guise of "government services." They ushered in a new era of sweetheart deals that kept the politicians in power and their financial supporters fat, happy and "protected." Sound familiar? Over the years, the federal government started gradually reaching into our personal lives by way of selling these schemes as "helping the people." So now the federal government has their far-reaching tentacles in almost every area of our personal and business lives: healthcare, housing, family, forced "retirement" Ponzi scheme (a.k.a. Social Security), welfare and education. They have even forced their way into deciding who we can and can't marry! And they have failed at all of them . . . miserably.

Granted, as the country has grown and prospered, there are additional services that are needed, such as the EPA, FDA and a few others. But all of those well-meaning departments, agencies and programs, and the regulations they enforce, have become totally out of control because there is virtually ZERO oversight. They are managed by bureaucrats who answer to no one directly, and, because they are represented by the government workers' unions, are impossible to get rid of. Sadly, they make up over 80% of the federal government.

We are not talking about Military, Monetary, Postal and Judicial. We are talking about just the overreaching, out-of-control departments, agencies and programs.

The Common Sense 80% plan would shut down these excessive programs entirely. Those that are truly necessary would be put back in the hands of the individual states. But how do we make that happen? How do we tear apart the big, fat, bloated bureaucracy, hand the power back to the states and still receive the benefit and "value" of the services that we have already paid into over the years? We take the management of these services away from the bureaucrats and we return the power to the states and/or local governments to oversee.

Is it as easy as it sounds? Could we do it? How could we, for example, possibly dismantle an agency as large as the EPA with a budget in excess of $8 billion and over 15,000 employees?

It is possible. In fact, it's been going on in the private sector for quite some time. Anyone who is familiar with the concept of a co-op, or cooperative, understands this. A co-op comes in many forms such as Farm Bureau or Home Owners Associations. A co-op is unique in that they are typically managed close to home, run more efficiently and require personal accountability by their members, board and management. They are generally funded by members and managed by a group of people, (typically a board of directors or trustees), that are elected or appointed by the members. Most are well-managed and watched like a hawk because the members have full transparency of the operation and finances of the entity.

Could such a system work for our expansive federal agencies?

Beyond Military, Monetary, Postal and Judicial, there are some agencies that a modern society needs. But most can simply go away. Indeed, nearly all of them start off as well-meaning endeavors but quickly turn into pork barrel projects, pushed through by a politician who is getting greased by the beneficiaries of the endeavor. The "endeavor" gets money appropriated to fund it, then it gets an appointed department, agency or program head to manage it. These managers, in many cases, have very little or even no experience in the area of "service" they are supposed to be running. Typically, they are bureaucrats working their way up the government food chain, or they are owed a political favor. It's like cancer in its early stages. At Stage 1, the symptoms remain undetectable. Once the cells begin to grow and replicate, the cancer multiplies rapidly. In the case of the new government endeavor, with virtually no direct accountable supervision, it fights for more and more funding to grow.

The cancer spreads and turns into Stage 2. At this point, the endeavor has nothing to do with serving the public or sometimes even the "purpose" for which it was started. Its primary purpose has metastasized into maneuvering for every dollar it can get.

At Stage 3, it's only about job security for the people who now depend on the cancerous budget. They will do anything in their power to survive. It slips into full malignant Stage 4 and becomes yet another bureaucratic cancer that has weakened our country to the point of death. It is now so complicated and embedded that it is almost impossible to shut down.

What do these cancers feed on? It's easy to follow the money when you read stories about the end-of-year funding requests for equipment, supplies and unnecessary new hires that go wasted and unused by these various departments, agencies and programs. For brevity, let's refer to them as "the cancers." These end-of-year purchases and new hires are made not because the department needs them. They are made so that the cancers will get a nice, fat budget increase and won't lose their funding or have it reduced the next year.

One of my good friends worked at the Department of Labor as her first job out of her MBA program at George Washington University. During the four years she was there, she was constantly reminded that her work output was too fast and that the ability to output that much work could cause them to lose funding for "next year's budget." Every year, her direct manager had her order a new laptop and other unnecessary equipment and supplies. She already had a laptop that was new when she started the job, and then two more from year-end ordering sprees that remained unopened. When it was time to order laptop number four, she had had enough. She could no longer tolerate the inefficiency, corruption and lack of accountability.

Multiply this tiny example by the thousands of examples and by the thousands of people in this SINGLE department. Then, if you can, imagine that number multiplied by the millions. Years of unnecessary and wasteful spending by millions of people in hundreds of thousands of budgets.

Our bureaucracies, well-intentioned or not, end up out of control.

Let's talk about how we can shut down most of the "cancers" of the federal government and create a system with responsible management, while providing much-needed services to the people of our great country. It is relatively easy to sort out what cancers stay or go at the federal level. Unless it is Military, Monetary, Postal or Judicial, it is likely that the "service" provided by the "cancer" can be administered much more efficiently on a state or local level. Keep the money and management close to home where personal accountability means something.

It's time to aggressively treat this cancer and wipe it out for good. Let the chemo begin!

Here's the challenge: There are departments whose "services" require national cooperation between the states, such as the EPA, Interior, Transportation, etc. Presently, each of these departments has appointed figurehead "Directors" or "Secretaries." But, beneath the surface, they are all irresponsibly managed by bureaucrats—nameless, faceless bureaucrats that are impossible to get rid of.

These bureaucrats usually stay in their positions for many years over the course of multiple administrations. They become more and more entrenched every day they are there, making it virtually impossible for them to be replaced, even by new administrations who don't necessarily share the same governing views and philosophies. It is a web that is so entangled the only way to shut it down is to literally "shut it down" and reform these departments and agencies in a way that can be managed by the people. The administrative structure has to be one that truly represents the people, states and municipalities.

Again, one of the biggest problems with these departments is that, beneath the surface, many of them are made up of people who have zero practical experience in the area in which they serve. This is where the co-op management structure comes into play. For example, let's take the Department of Interior. No, it is not in charge of picking out carpet and drapes. For the most part, the DOI is in charge of managing government-owned land and properties. You may have read some of the horror stories over the years about their overreach, like literally taking private land without cause, the gross mismanagement of government properties, and even the big "Sex for Oil" scandal. The bottom line is, someone has to manage the land and property that is owned by the federal government. The key word there is "manage." As with most of the federal departments, the Department of Interior (under the Bush, Sr., Clinton, Bush, Jr., and especially Obama administrations) has grown into an ill-managed bureaucratic nightmare, with those in charge having little accountability for their actions. They are entrenched, and they know that they are there for as long as they want to be. And they have (up until recently) very little actual oversight.

The patterns are obvious. These departments take on a life of their own and have almost zero representation of the states. That's how they get away with some of their questionable actions, and how they quietly sneak in these ridiculous over-reaching regulations and unnecessary year-end budget requests. They have almost no oversight.

To save our country, let's restructure the majority of these departments, programs and agencies so that there is direct representation of and by the states. We can install a system of accountability so the power is always rotated and there is intense fiscal and administrative oversight.

How? The bureaucrats and the establishment Congressional members are going to hate this, but I think you'll like it. Radical? Maybe. Easy to implement? YES!

Each necessary service, including the Department of Interior, Environmental Protection Agency, Department of Transportation and Federal Communications Commission, becomes an independent entity in the form of co-op and operates outside of the direct supervision of the federal government. It should have its own detailed operating budget, shared and funded by the states, and management structures that put personal accountability front and center.

States can choose whether they want to participate or not depending on their own needs. Each state appoints two trustees, making a board of trustees for each entity. The states can appoint them as they wish. Ideally, the state governors would nominate the trustees from their state with the approval of the state legislatures. These appointees must be independent individuals with a certain level of expertise and practical experience in the field of the entity's focus. For instance, for the Department of Interior, individuals with experience in real estate management, mineral rights management or parks and recreation might be an excellent choice. For the Department of Transportation, individuals with expertise in the business of air travel, road construction and engineering would be the way to go.

With each entity having a co-op board of trustees that is made up of private citizens from across the country, it will bring a wide variety of real-world practical views, actionable ideas and management skills. Most importantly, we the people will have actual representation within the entity. If there is an issue, we have a name and face from our own state to call.

How do we recapture the value of the "services" and accounts that we have already paid for? In other words, how do we get back the money that we have paid in over the years to the likes of Medicare and Social Security?

We have all paid into these ridiculous schemes. With the way our government is operating, most of us will never realize even a fraction of the value of our forced "investment." However, we have paid in and deserve to get the full benefit. For lack of a better term, the government owes us restitution for the money they have taken from us. It is easier than you think to recover this money when you apply the Common Sense 80% solution. As you go through this book, we will address how to get the full value of our investment and collect our rightfully owed restitution.

Keep in mind as you read the following pages that WE are the ones who will be either running for office, recruiting people to run for office and/or supporting someone who will run for office. So go ahead and take some notes. You, or someone you know, may soon be leading the charge!

Our candidates could run with one commonality, whether they are Republicans, Democrats or Independents. Our candidates will run supporting the Common Sense 80% platform. And they will sign a pledge to strictly vote and support the Common Sense 80% platform without compromise. To be sure they keep their word, they will place a letter of resignation in escrow that can be pulled out and filed if they step out of line. Crazy? Maybe. But it will force elected officials to honor their word and NEVER compromise.

There are 435 House seats and 100 Senate seats which, for the most part, are unnecessarily filled with career politicians.

It's time to take a stand and take action. Are you ready?

Chapter Three

Federal Spending: Lack of Accountability

—〰—

"A body of men holding themselves accountable to nobody ought not to be trusted by anybody."

—Thomas Paine

The federal government contains over 1,000 existing federal agencies, departments and programs, employs approximately 3 million people, and spends around $4 trillion of our money every year. This amount represents $12,000 spent on every man, woman and child in the United States.

For many people, envisioning $4 trillion may be difficult to comprehend.

It is—and that's the problem.

If that isn't enough to make your head spin, consider the debt. At $20.6 trillion, each citizen's share of that debt is in excess of over $138,000 per taxpayer. This debt is rising at an exponential rate and projected to approach $30 trillion by 2023!

With no concept of accountability or foresight, our lawmakers are driving our country into an unrecoverable death spiral of spending and debt. So how did our great country go from virtually zero debt and deficit to almost insolvency?

From 1789 to 1860 the federal government was lean and performing pretty much the way it was designed. Because our Founding Fathers built the country on a blueprint of sound principles, there was nary a debt and almost always a surplus. (Spending less than we take in and have savings for a rainy day. What a concept! Thanks, Ben Franklin!) The first time the federal budget exceeded $1 billion was in 1865, the year the Civil War ended. The cost of war, of course, has always taken its toll on government spending. In fact, after the two world wars, the nation's spike in spending continued to explode as we poured our resources and public debt into gunpowder, aluminum and infrastructure. After each of these major conflicts, spending dropped to near, but never equal, prewar levels. This resulted in a cumulative increase over time. But, as postwar reconstruction affected GDP, our economy always saw a significant boost in economic health right along with that slight increase in spending... until the Vietnam War.

Year	Expenditures	Year	Expenditures
1800	$11,000,000	1970	$195,649,000,000
1805	$10,088,000	1975	$332,332,000,000
1810	$8,700,000	1980	$590,941,000,000
1815	$33,500,000	1985	$946,344,000,000
1820	$19,400,000	1990	$1,252,990,000,000
1825	$17,100,000	1995	$1,515,740,000,000
1830	$17,100,000	2000	$1,788,950,000,000
1835	$20,300,000	2001	$1,862,850,000,000
1840	$29,000,000	2002	$2,010,890,000,000
1845	$27,300,000	2003	$2,159,900,000,000
1850	$44,800,000	2004	$2,292,840,000,000
1855	No data found	2005	$2,471,960,000,000

1860	$78,000,000	2006	$2,655,050,000,000
1865	$1,311,000,000	2007	$2,728,690,000,000
1870	$334,000,000	2008	$2,982,540,000,000
1875	$308,000,000	2009	$3,517,680,000,000
1880	$304,000,000	2010	$3,457,080,000,000
1885	$310,000,000	2011	$3,603,060,000,000
1890	$384,000,000	2012	$3,536,940,000,000
1895	$443,000,000	2013	$3,454,650,000,000
1900	$629,000,000	2014	$3,506,090,000,000
1905	$661,000,000	2015	$3,690,000,000,000
1910	$840,000,000	2016	$3,850,000,000,000
1915	$1,051,000,000	2017	$4,060,000,000,000
1920	$6,785,000,000		
1925	$3,623,000,000		
1930	$3,956,000,000		
1935	$7,553,000,000		
1940	$10,061,000,000		
1945	$106,877,000,000		
1950	$44,800,000,000		
1955	$73,441,000,000		
1960	$97,000,000,000		
1965	$118,228,000,000		

After the Vietnam War concluded, for the first time in our nation's history, expenditures increased. The main reason for this increase in spending was the introduction of massive "hand-out" programs, otherwise dubbed as "entitlement" programs. LBJ's "War on Poverty" programs weren't satisfied with Social Security and the properly funded pension programs for America's non-working and working folk. He further compounded what was already a disaster waiting to happen, by adding Medicaid and Medicare to the mix.

Here is an analytical view of the growth of federal spending. Take a look at the years and consider what was happening during those times.

(Budget/Spending in Millions)

Year	Receipts	Outlays	Surplus/Deficit
1960	$531,000,000,000	$530,000,000,000	$1,730,000,000
1965	$628,000,000,000	$636,000,000,000	-$7,590,000,000
1970	$864,000,000,000	$877,000,000,000	-$12,700,000,000
1975	$922,000,000,000	$1,100,000,000,000	-$176,000,000,000
1980	$1,190,000,000,000	$1,360,000,000,000	-$170,000,000,000
1985	$1,290,000,000,000	$1,660,000,000,000	-$373,000,000,000
1990	$1,560,000,000,000	$1,890,000,000,000	-$334,000,000,000
1995	N/A	N/A	N/A
2000	$2,490,000,000,000	$2,200,000,000,000	$290,000,000,000
2001	$2,390,000,000,000	$2,220,000,000,000	$154,000,000,000
2002	$2,190,000,000,000	$2,370,000,000,000	-$186,000,000,000
2003	$2,060,000,000,000	$2,500,000,000,000	-$437,000,000,000
2004	$2,120,000,000,000	$2,590,000,000,000	-$466,000,000,000
2005	$2,360,000,000,000	$2,710,000,000,000	-$349,000,000,000
2006	$2,550,000,000,000	$2,820,000,000,000	-$263,000,000,000
2007	$2,650,000,000,000	$2,820,000,000,000	-$166,000,000,000
2008	$2,550,000,000,000	$3,0200,000,000,000	-$464,000,000,000

2009	$2,100,000,000,000	$3,520,000,000,000	-$1,410,000,000,000
2010	$2,140,000,000,000	$3,430,000,000,000	-$1,280,000,000,000
2011	$2,240,000,000,000	$3,500,000,000,000	-$1,260,000,000,000
2012	$2,340,000,000,000	$3,370,000,000,000	-$1,040,000,000,000
2013	$2,600,000,000,000	$3,240,000,000,000	-$637,000,000,000
2014	$2,790,000,000,000	$3,230,000,000,000	-$447,000,000,000

Regarding deficits, we have always run a deficit during wars. The Civil War pushed our country into its first major budget deficit of a whopping -$990 million that continued until the surplus during the Roaring '20s. World War II pushed our deficits into the billions with a peak of over -$47 billion that remained until our surpluses of the '60s.

Why is this trend disturbing? Since the end of the Vietnam War, our deficits have shown only one brief moment of reprieve. Thanks to President Bill Clinton and the Newt Gingrichled Congress, helped along by the ridiculous distractions of personal issues with the executive branch (insert cigar joke here), we did show a surplus for a very brief moment in 2000.

After 2000, the trend has since returned to running a massive annual deficit, even exceeding ONE TRILLION in some years. And that's *Trillion* with a T! We are drifting year after year without sufficient money to run our government.

The interest alone exceeds our annual budget of just twenty years ago. According to our friends at usdebtclock.org, our current federal debt as of Q2 2019 is a whopping **$22,300,000,000,000** and is increasing daily. That amount is only what is classified as "Current Debt." That doesn't count the additional debt that is classified as "Unfunded liabilities." Unfunded liabilities are actual debts and obligations, primarily owed to us—you and me—in the form of Social Security, Medicare, etc. And that debt is over five times the amount of the "current debt." It is a whopping $124,000,000,000,000, and it is real! (Do you see how many zeroes there are?!?)

With this continuation of spending and committing money that we don't have—the current debt of almost $22 TRILLION, the interest racking up on that debt along with $124 TRILLION in "unfunded liabilities"— it is obvious that our current bunch of "lawmakers" doesn't have the intestinal fortitude to step up, be responsible and face the music that they, themselves, composed. Immediate cutting will likely be painful at first. But, as soon as we start drastically trimming away and getting the spending, waste and bureaucracy under control, a more lean and efficient service-oriented government will emerge.

Why hasn't this happened yet? Because the members of Congress live and die by how much money they raise, making them WAY too beholden to their sugar-daddy lobbyists, big corporations, special interest groups and party leaders to do anything that would be out of step with their wishes. Big pharmaceutical corporations, unions, insurance companies, telecom companies, mega-banks, you name it.

Our lawmakers, by "necessity," have to support legislation that allows the big corporations and other special interests, (who already pick our pockets daily), to continue to dig deeper into our pockets while at the same time steer our country into financial ruin. In other words, our establishment elected officials have become "bitches to the man."

Over the years, many activists have suggested minor across-the-board government spending cuts of 10–15 percent, just like what many households and small businesses have to do when they overspend their way into out-of-control debt and operating costs.

Total Spending FY2013

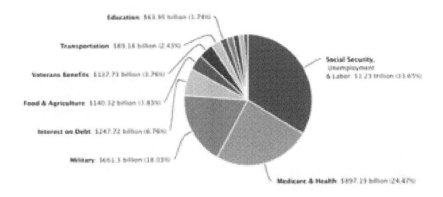

But really? 10–15%? That's only a drop in a very, very large bucket. A 10–15% cut is like pissing in the ocean. Any such modest cut wouldn't make a dent in our government's financial woes. Why do our lawmakers feel they are immune from paying back borrowed money? Why are they allowed to run massive debt with no accountability?

I am so amused when a politician brags that his or her "bill" cut $3 million in spending. That number for any individual taxpayer or small businessperson seems formidable. Three million dollars is a lot of money for anyone, right? Not for the government.

First of all, when politicians brag about their spending cut, it is quite often not a cut at all. It is likely a cut in the *rate of spending* or a cut in proposed spending (a.k.a. Congressional speak for absolute horse shit).

In the unlikely event a spending cut is actually a real cut in spending, let's put it into perspective:

National Debt:	$ 22,379,136,000,000+ (and growing)
Unfunded Liabilities (debt)	$124,415,730,000,000+ (and growing)
Total Actual Debt:	$146,794,866,000,000
Spending Cut:	$3,000,000
New Debt (after spending cut):	$146,794,863,000,000

Brilliant! Now, instead of $146,794,866,000,000 in debt, we only have $146,794,863,000,000. Hooray!

Oops, one problem.

In the time you took to read this paragraph, the interest on that current debt of $20.6 trillion has already well exceeded the $3 million saved. You see, $3 million is actually a very, very small number. The national debt increases approximately $4.5 million every minute of every day. Rain or shine, night or day, that debt keeps piling on and compounding.

The annual interest on our current debt is $458,542,287,311. WOWZA! If you want to visualize this sickening debt growth in real time along with the rest of the government's sickening financial stats, visit usdebtclock. org. It is mind-warping, to say the least!

But for now, let's stay focused on the 50,000-foot view. It gets even more discouraging when you add the following facts. In addition to the current debt of over $22.3 trillion, the "Einsteins" in Congress approved spending that exceeded its income by approximately $800 billion (the deficit):

2017 income:	$3,200,000,000,000
2017 spending	$4,000,000,000,000
(LOSS)	($800,000,000,000)

Yes, folks, "our" government spent approximately $800 BILLION more than it collected in 2017. And again, let's repeat in BOLD. **There are those additional "off the books" obligations (debt) they call unfunded liabilities of over $110 trillion (Social Security, Medicare, etc.).** These obligations should concern us the most. Why? Because the overwhelming majority of them are, in reality, debts owed to us. That is money that you and I have paid in and are likely never to receive. Those obligations are not just pieces of paper. It is money that is supposed to cover our Medicare, Social Security and the likes thereof. This is all very alarming as these programs are failing and becoming more insolvent year by year even if we, the people, continue to pay for these programs.

The obligations are real, they are owed to us, and the payouts from these programs are growing as our population ages, lives longer, gets lazier and becomes more dependent on government assistance. If it weren't for the ability of the federal government to keep printing money, they couldn't begin to make good on those obligations. And "growing" our way out of debt is no longer an option. How do we 'spend' our way back to solvency? Maybe they are counting on doing the same thing they did in that old Saturday Night Live "change bank" sketch. But how do we make money? One word: Volume!

Just in case you missed it, let's review:

National Debt:	$ 22,300,000,000,000+
Unfunded Liabilities (debt)	$124,400,000,000,000+
Total Actual Debt:	$146,700,000,000,000+

Don't believe that this is a problem? Take a look at the numbers again and try to make the case that we can "spend" our way out of this ever-deepening hole.

Share the numbers with any fifth-grade math student or MBA of Finance and ask him or her what it will take to reverse this trend. (Hint: Anything less than an immediate, bold overhaul won't work.)

Billions and trillions are pretty overwhelming numbers. No matter how you stack them up or manipulate them, the government's current financial woes are bleak at best. To make the numbers easier to wrap our heads around for folks like you and me, let's take the above example of the United States government's debt, deficit, income and expenditures and look at it as though it were a family having to manage its own finances. To get the numbers down to figures we can relate to, let's remove eight zeros from the end of the numbers so we can easily see how these numbers would stack up if we were a typical family. Let's call them "the Joneses." (Fasten your seatbelts because this is going to be a short, simple, but unbelievably wild ride through a VERY poorly managed family budget.)

Here is the current financial state of America as "The Joneses" in 2017:

Jones annual income:	$32,000
Jones annual spending	$40,000
Income after expenses:	-$8,000 (LOSS)
Current family debt:	$206,000
2017 new debt (a.k.a. deficit):	$8,000
Other obligations (unfunded liabilities):	$1,100,000
FAMILY TOTAL DEBT AT YEAR END 2017:	**$1,414,000**

Imagine a family that has racked up over $206,000 in current debt, has additional outstanding obligations of $1,100,000, is currently on track this year to spend $8,000 more than they bring in, and whose gross annual income is still only at $32,000. Does that financial situation sound stable to you? Do you think you could go to the bank and ask for a loan with a straight face while your finances are in such shambles?

Let's expand this nightmare. Suppose a large portion of this family's debt is owed to an unfriendly neighbor who, despite so, is a provider of most of the products this family consumes. Let us say this neighbor is well financed and has a very well thought out long-term perspective on his personal growth (i.e. China and Saudi Arabia). Oh, and let's not miss the fact that this neighbor's family owns not only the debt but is about to jack up the interest rates on that debt over the next few years. Are they hoping you win the lotto and pay them off? No way! Their dream is to see you fail miserably so they can own you—lock, stock and barrel.

As responsible, accountable and productive individuals, we are mindful of our income and expenses. Sure, there are times when we take on debt like buying a house.

However, that debt is never an obligation taken on without adequate collateral and a clear and present method of repayment. Any business-person will tell you that debt, without a clear and bountiful method of repayment, dramatically increases the chances of failure. As individual citizens, our families' budgets and our small businesses' budgets have one failsafe mechanism that protects us from financial ruin: **Accountability.**

When we are accountable to our budget, we marshal all our efforts to the two things that we can control and manage. We can always control our expenses and, if we are not lazy, we can certainly make as much money as we want in America. The old saying goes, "If you can measure it, you can manage it." Congress oversees the budget but the only thing Congress has managed over the past 30 years is lining up money for their next election.

The only solution that has a snowball's chance in hell of bringing America back to its glory as a world leader in innovation, financial strength and military defense is a radical solution. It is so radical yet simple that most people will dismiss it as pure folly. Ready? Here it is. Don't blink or you'll miss it!

Solution: Stay on Budget and Let the States Provide.

Require the government to only spend what it brings in and shift all non-federal services (i.e., health, education, welfare and housing) to the states.

I challenge anyone to show me where the federal government is a more efficient delivery system of services. When it comes to health, labor, education, the arts, emergency services, or any of the 99% of current federal departments, local, regional, and state governments can do a better, more efficient and more responsible job. The further our tax money travels from our homes, the less efficient that money becomes. The federal government's responsibility should be limited to what it is limited to in the Constitution:

1. Defend our soil against other countries and terrorists.

2. Manage the monetary system.

3. Manage and maintain postal services.

4. Strictly enforce the Constitution ONLY with a federal judicial system.

In 1995, we came within a single vote in the Senate of passing a "Contract with America" that would have been a first step toward easing the tsunami of debt that the politicians and bureaucrats have incurred on our behalf. Since the "good ol' boys" on Capitol Hill are reluctant to be accountable, we need to become keenly aware of the crisis our lawmakers (as puppets of the corporation-lobbyist-union-bureaucrat quartet) have put us in. We need TRUE and ACCOUNTABLE leadership. In other words, we need brave new leadership. We need citizen statesmen who are true to their word and the "Agreement" outlined in this book.

Our United States and the freedom that we enjoy as Americans are fading quickly.

Alarmist? Nope. It's happened before:

"Call the United States what you like—superpower, hegemon or empire—but its ability to manage its finances is closely tied to its ability to remain the predominant global military power...

This is how empires decline. It begins with a debt explosion. It ends with an inexorable reduction in the resources available for the Army, Navy and Air Force...

If the United States doesn't come up soon with a credible plan to restore the federal budget to balance over the next five to ten years, the danger is very real that a debt crisis could lead to a major weakening of American power.

The precedents are certainly there. Habsburg, Spain, defaulted on all or part of its debt fourteen times between 1557 and 1696 and also succumbed to inflation due to a surfeit of New World silver. Pre-revolutionary France was spending 62 percent of royal revenue on debt service by 1788.

The Ottoman Empire went the same way: interest payments and amortization rose from 15 percent of the budget in 1860 to 50 percent in 1875. And don't forget the last great English-speaking empire. By the interwar years, interest payments were consuming 44 percent of the British budget, making it intensely difficult to rearm in the face of a new German threat.

Call it the fatal arithmetic of imperial decline. Without radical fiscal reform, it could apply to America next."

—Naill Ferguson, Historian. (*Newsweek,* Nov. 27, 2009)

When it comes to a "litmus test" for federal or state responsibility, the logic is irrefutable:

A) The federal government has no business involving itself in social issues, religious or otherwise.

B) Whatever the states and local governments can handle should be handled at state and local levels where leaders can be held accountable. Note that states and local governments can handle nearly everything except defense, transportation, our monetary system and judicial cases dealing with constitutional issues.

You should understand by now that, with only a few exceptions, the closer to home your dollars stay, the better those dollars are managed.

Why? Because your local city councilman has to see you face to face on a regular basis, whether it is at church, a high school ballgame or the Kiwanis pancake breakfast. Your local councilman is fully accountable to you. He can't hide behind a bunch of faceless bureaucrats in Washington. In the appendix section, after "Take ACTION," we outline each federal department, one by one. Read this list and ask yourself what the country would look like without the burden of a $3.21 trillion budget and the over 3 million bureaucrats who are fueled by it. Imagine your local leaders, friends and neighbors handling most of those necessary functions at the state or local level. Those in need would be taken care of properly by those who care: their community. Businesses would have the freedom to start up, grow, hire more people and pump fresh money back into the economy. Picture a happy, healthy and prosperous country that is not bogged down by overreaching regulations and red tape. Let us give the power back to the state and local governments to get rid of unnecessary bureaucrats and stop the nonsense completely.

It may seem like this is an idea that is too extreme or too disruptive to implement. However, if you think getting a shot of Novocain is painful, try to get your teeth pulled with no anesthetic at all!

Like the Ottoman, Roman and dozens of other empires before ours, our once great United States and its unparalleled achievement of abundance and opportunity is headed for the history museums of 2021 if we don't take decisive and massive action now.

We can stop adding in ridiculous earmarks that spend our money on silly programs that do nothing. We can stop the $27 million spent on teaching Moroccans how to teach pottery to each other to improve *their* economy. We could probably have done without the National Science Foundation spending $516,000 on a video game called Prom Week. The $35,600,000 spent to subsidize an unused trolley system in Saint Louis that covers 2.2 miles could have been spent better or not spent at all.

Perhaps the Pakistanis would object if we cut back on spending, though; we spent $30,000,000 to promote the sales of mangoes from Pakistani farmers and $10,000,000 to create a Pakistani Sesame Street. The federal government wasted $3,000,000 via the National Science Foundation on studying how long shrimp can run on a treadmill. Really?! Why? Are they planning on regulating shrimp endurance?

Maybe. Who knows?

Just the fact that they somehow justify these outrageous expenditures is beyond ridiculous. Someone's getting rich on our nickel, and you and I are getting zero benefits. I'm sure the shrimp treadmill factory is in full swing, leading the world in shrimp endurance technology. My old buddy Bill Lowery was right when he would say, "Brilliant! F***ing brilliant! Your government at work for you!"

Chapter Four

"We're From the IRS and
We Are Here to Help"

—⚏—

*"It is a good thing that we don't get as much government
as we pay for."*

—**Will Rogers**

In order to fund the Union during the Civil War, President Abraham Lincoln and Congress imposed the first income tax (see Revenue Act of 1861). The next year they levied more taxes for war expenses and created the office of Commissioner of Internal Revenue (see Revenue Act of 1862). The position of commissioner exists today as the head of the Internal Revenue Service. The Revenue Act of 1862 was passed as an emergency and temporary wartime tax. It copied a relatively new British system of income taxation, instead of trade and property taxation. Here's how it went:

- The initial rate was 3% on income over $800, which exempted most wage earners. Adjusted for inflation, this represented an annual federal income tax of approximately $900 for a family earning over $30,000.

- In 1862, the rate was 3% on income between $600 and $10,000, and 5% on income over $10,000.

- In 1864, the rate was 5% on income between $600 and $5,000; 7.5% on income $5,000–$10,000; and 10% on income $10,000 and above. By the end of the war, 10% of Union households had paid some form of income tax, which accounted for 21% of the Union's war funding. The income tax was repealed ten years later in 1871. Congress revived the income tax in 1894, but the Supreme Court ruled it unconstitutional the following year.

Then, in 1913, Wyoming ratified the Sixteenth Amendment, providing the three-fourths majority of states necessary to amend the Constitution. The Sixteenth Amendment gave Congress the authority to enact an income tax.

That same year, the first Form 1040 appeared after Congress levied a 1% tax—yep! One percent!—on net personal incomes above $3,000. Adjusted for inflation, a $3,000 annual income in 1913 represents over $74,166 in 2017. In 1918, during World War I, the top rate of the income tax rose to 77% to help finance the war effort. It dropped sharply in the postwar years, down to 24% in 1929, but it rose again during the Great Depression.

During World War II, Congress introduced payroll withholding and quarterly tax payments.

Today, the size, scope, power and infrastructure to support the IRS is nearly unimaginable. The Obama administration's 2016 budget request for the Internal Revenue Service was nearly $13,922,269,000, an increase of $1,946,322,000 from the Fiscal Year 2015 budget. That is $13.9 billion of our money used to collect more of our money. And honestly, with a budget of $13.9 billion, why the hell can't I get an agent on the phone when I have a question? Were you having the same thought?

That $13.9 billion is used merely to collect and account for the federal income tax. Keep that figure in mind as we present the common-sense solution to funding and running a lean, purposeful and effective federal government.

During FY 2015, the IRS processed $243.3 million federal tax returns and supplemental documents and collected $3.3 trillion in gross taxes. After accounting for $199 million refunds, totaling $403.3 billion, collections (net of refunds) totaled $1.8 trillion.

Also during FY 2015, there were more than 163.5 million individual income tax returns filed, accounting for 78.2% of all returns filed. Individual income tax withheld and tax payments, combined, totaled almost $1.8 trillion before refunds.

Additionally, the number of resources comprising time, infrastructure, accounting and support services (money it costs us to hire "professionals" to interpret the tax code so we can file a return) is reported to be in excess of $300 billion. IRS agents can earn $48,000 to $150,000 per year in salary. A recent Bureau of Economic Analysis report showed that all federal employees, on average, earn approximately 40–55% more than their counterparts in the private sector.

For instance, if you're a middle management executive working in the private sector, you're probably making around $60,000 per year. A lot is expected of you and you are held accountable for your productivity. Meanwhile, a government employee, and a much less productive person with an "equal" position, likely exceeds $86,635 annually. Add in the benefits and it could exceed $123,049, compared to just $70,081 for the private sector. They receive better benefits that, thanks to the government workers' unions, include a pension plan that allows a federal government worker to retire at any age with at least 25 years' creditable federal service . . . with a HUGE bloated pension. In other words, if you are a private sector employee, statistically, you are likely doing three times the amount of work and getting paid half as much. Makes you want to cringe, vomit or both.

Are you following this? Does anyone understand what a trillion dollars represents? How about a billion? The numbers are so large that our brains cannot comprehend what the impact is. We'll break down the actual budget by department agencies and programs later, so you can see where our money is going.

The IRS employs approximately 115,000 people. Payroll, offices (much of which is class "A" office space), IT infrastructure, pensions, utilities and support for this behemoth department increase the overall expense dramatically. What is this entire infrastructure for? Obviously, it is necessary to interpret, administer and enforce the tax code. And who understands the tax code? Nobody.

During the 26-year period from 1913 to 1939, the IRS tax code went from a few pages to a whopping 400–500 pages. Think of it as a drier version of the book War and Peace. After the Great Depression, FDR's "New Deal," and World War II, the pages mushroomed to over 8,000. That is an increase of over 1,600%! If you think that is bad, consider that currently, the U.S. tax code is 74,608 pages, which is 187 times longer than the 1930s-era tax code.

In "government-speak," the rate of increase in the tax code has dropped by almost half with an increase of only 900% since 1939. Woohoo! A reduction in the rate means nothing. The paper continues to multiply like a colony of rabbits. The number of confusing hurdles, complex formulas, confusing exceptions, pork barrel-based credits and deductions is impossible for any single person to comprehend.

No corporation (nonprofit or otherwise) would stand for such incredible waste. Why have we given our government any latitude on accountability?

In 1980 Congress passed the Paperwork Reduction Act. Among its purposes was to minimize the paperwork burden for individuals, small businesses, educational and nonprofit institutions, federal contractors, state, local and tribal governments and other persons, resulting from the collection of information by or for the federal government. Sounds like a good idea, right?

Wrong.

You see, it's who designs a system like this that matters. When the people (the same ones who generate over 74,000 incomprehensible pages of "code" with which to tax us), come up with an idea to reduce paperwork, the outcome should be relatively predictable.

We learned from the government Office of Management and Budget (OMB) that for the fiscal year 2015, it only took us, individuals and small business owners, 11.5 billion hours to fill out "government paperwork." With 120 million households, an average of a forty-hour work week, that is nearly two weeks of our lives devoted to complying with red tape. That figure is down from FY2009 when we consumed approximately 10 billion hours. That decline sounds good until we learn that most of the decline is because federal agencies decided that it really didn't take you as long to fill out forms as they thought it did, so they conveniently adjusted it in their favor without any basis whatsoever.

Why?

On the "Blame Bush" front, large increases were reported between 2002 and 2005, but much of that increase was the result of the advent of the Medicare Prescription Drug Program—increasing the "busy work" hours by 250 million. If you have a hard time imagining 250 million hours, that equates to over 28,522 years.

On the "Blame Obama" front, the biggest single-year jump in the past decade came in 2010, when individuals and businesses spent an extra 352 million hours responding to documentation requests from agencies prompted by new statutory requirements. For example, in 2011, it was reported that employers needed almost 70 million additional hours to claim a new credit for hiring more workers. Restaurants spent 14.5 million hours to display calorie counts for their menus, most of which vary so much that accuracy is impossible even by make-believe government standards. But by far, the largest increase goes to the Securities and Exchange Commission, not because it added more forms, but because it decided that filling out forms took twice as long.

What the OMB doesn't state is how many man hours the government spent figuring out how many man hours individuals and businesses spent sending paperwork to Washington. I guess that should be added in as well.

Although, at this point, does it really matter? The tax code and its enforcement are a tangled web of regulations that are so complicated that even the IRS "help" line will give you a different interpretation of the same rule and regulations. That is, if you can get them on the phone.

If someone walked up to you, flashed a gun and an IRS badge and said, "I'm from the IRS. You are under arrest for violating article 257-B of the IRS tax code 2012 Section 23, Article 45, Paragraph 8," could you put up a defensible argument?

How could any taxpayer or even a CPA team possibly comprehend, manage and dispense organizational action based on 74,000+ pages of gobbledygook when the IRS's agents can't uniformly interpret it? Check for yourself. Take any section of the government's complex tax code and call up five different IRS offices, and I will bet you'll get five different answers.

Do you think this is only a textbook example with no real-world consequences? Think again. In late 2011, Paul Hatz of Boston was knee-deep in appealing the results of a five-year-long "nightmare IRS audit."

According to Hatz, the auditor failed to send out statutory notice of deficiency letters—thus denying him 'the most fundamental taxpayer right, the right to appeal what an auditor says,' he said—and he was slapped with a personal lien for $110,000 in taxes and penalties. The liability, though, wasn't Hatz's, but rather that of the 'c' corporation he ran, which by definition is taxed separately from its proprietors. "To add insult to injury, this 'tax' was all because the auditor misclassified money I invested into the corporation as 'income,'" Hatz said. Because of the auditor's error, not only did Hatz lose the $100,000 investment he made in his corporation, he also got a bill from the IRS for $110,000 for failing to report the amount as income.

"I know this sounds crazy, and I wish I made it all up," Hatz said. Hatz hired a tax attorney and got a Congressman involved. But as a result of the financial burdens of the audit process, Hatz ended up closing his small manufacturing business, where he employed over a dozen people. Now he collects unemployment and takes care of his child as a stay-at-home dad while he looks for work. He's dropped $60,000 in CPA and tax attorney costs and had to declare bankruptcy. He and his spouse keep their finances separate nowadays. (Visit https://www.irs.com/articles/tax-horror-stories-will-give-you-nightmares for more stories.) This is one of the many examples where an out-of-control government screws up and over a dozen people are left out of work, businesses close and the manufacturing output of those businesses are likely being sent back to China.

The taxes our government collects continue to be both a barometer and a rudder. Politicians from both sides of the aisle use the threat of increased taxes and then project calamity if we don't "fix" the problem. Like all politicians, trained and controlled by the infected bunch of D.C. lobbyists and bureaucrats, they campaign on reform. But once the Bible is withdrawn from their hand and they are sworn into office, they are sucked into a system of zero accountability and have only two things on their mind: raising money and pleasing party leaders for the next election.

It's true. From the moment they take office, the only thing Congressional members are accountable to are the wallets of the K Street lobbyists and special interest groups that will provide them with the dough they need to get re-elected time and time again and become more entrenched in the corrupt bureaucratic entanglement that he or she likely originally went to D.C. to fight and bring down.

I asked a close friend of mine, who is now in his fourth term as a Congressman, if there was an actual room in a building in D.C. where they took freshman members of Congress to suck out the parts of their brains and souls that prompted them to become a public servant in the first place. He laughed and said, "There are many such rooms, beginning with the lobbyist offices on K Street and going all the way up the party leadership on both sides." Backdoor deals, lobbyist influence and dozens of other systems that are flat-out illegal in the private sector are "business as usual" in Washington, D.C. At the heart of all of these issues are money and political power grabs.

How programs are funded and whom they benefit create power structures that sound great on the surface, but do not serve our country. They cater only to the self-interests of those who have enough money to hire slick, high-priced, power-brokering lobbyists who are the central part of the system, which has forgotten that the money and freedom they are squandering BELONGS TO US.

Remember, you and I are paying for all of it. Not only are we paying for it, but we are also supporting it by casting a vote for an incumbent of either party and by allowing portions of our association, union and club dues to go to lobbyists so that they can put our money to work stoking the D.C. furnace.

The current death spiral of our nation is directly related to the manner in which we account for our governance. The more they waste, the more wasteful they become. The more we don't hold our lawmakers accountable, the less accountable they become. The checks and balances of our three branches (judicial, executive, legislative) would work reasonably well for passing laws if they kept each law simple enough for the average person to understand. Purposefully, they don't. And, there are no adequate checks and balances regarding the taxes levied and the spending that is occurring. The United States of America has dug a financial hole of debt so deep it may be too late to get out of it. However, for a very short window of time, the future of our country is still in our hands. The engine that drives this out-of-control machine is the desire to get re-elected and serve the special interests, which are primarily made up of the big corporations and unions that reap the benefits.

Yes, our country needs money to operate, but there is a better way to collect it and keep our freedom intact. If we don't dismantle (not reform) the IRS and the machine that overtaxes its citizens and spends more money than it takes in, we will experience a full-on collapse and, to make it worse, America and the freedom it values will become the laughingstock of the naysayers like China and Saudi Arabia. It is time to face the music.

The United States is insolvent.

A financial collapse is imminent. In reality, it's already upon us. The sad fact is that nobody has the balls to step up, reveal the truth head-on and do something about it. It used to be that at least politicians "talked" a good game regarding reform. Until recently, all the political rhetoric (horseshit) they spew all sounded the same, and it was all taken song and verse, fed to them from their party leaders. But those days have come to an end. Regular people like you and me (non-establishment) are stepping up with strong talk and no-B.S. solutions.

The days of speaking in "sanitized" sound bites are over.

Today's sound bite politics is much the same as disco. It's all the same song and dance, in theory. It's just not as much fun, and it doesn't go as well with leisure suits and white guys with Afros.

While millions of families were cutting back, and businesses looked under every nook and cranny to seek out a profit, under Obama, the IRS sought a $944.5 million increase in its budget. While people like Paul Hatz look to survive after being destroyed by irresponsible government agents, the IRS is planning on nearly a billion dollars in new hires to execute antiquated collection systems, support confusing laws and enforce a new healthcare policy that nobody understands—including those who allegedly wrote it.

"Insanity: doing the same thing over and over again and expecting different results."

–Albert Einstein

I don't know what you call something that doesn't work, and we keep fueling it with more power and money. What is beyond insane? We need a new word.

Better than a new word for extreme insanity would be a logical, fair and seamless system to generate revenue for our government efficiently without a 74,000-page document to attempt to implement it. We can't seriously reform the IRS or the tax code as it is.

Trying to trim a budget or "fix" a system like the IRS makes about as much sense as giving a killer grizzly bear a manicure. It won't change him, and he will not be inclined to participate, anyway. We need to kill the bear.

Solution: Goodbye Income Tax and the IRS... Hello Consumption Tax.

Nobody enjoys paying taxes, especially on earnings. The majority of the tax code today has been written, re-written and modified for corporations and high-income earners to have loopholes and incentives to pay less (if not any) taxes. Both sides of the aisle spin and twist the tax code to the point where nobody truly knows anything. With a tax code that is impossible to understand, how can either side make an intelligent argument?

They can't.

When we dump the debilitating income tax in favor of a modest national sales tax, there will be no need for the IRS or its support services. This will also eliminate the need for most of the accounting and tax preparation expenses we currently incur. Sorry, H&R Block. Time to start retraining.

When we tax consumption instead of income, incomes will instantly increase. When incomes go up, spending and savings will also increase.

A national consumption tax would accomplish three major objectives:

1. We would eliminate 95% of the nation's tax collection efforts. The savings at the federal level would easily exceed hundreds of billions of expenditures annually. This would include dramatically reducing the expenditures needed to support the federal agency that oversees tax collection. The department's budget is a mere $11.7 billion, but the ripple effect of eliminating this department would be far-reaching, both in reducing the power of the federal government and the financial waste that is ruining our country.

2. A national sales tax would increase take-home income for the working-poor and middle-class. Most working- and middle-class families have limited or no tax deductions to reduce their income tax burden. With the elimination of FICA, SUTA, Social Security and the loop-holes that surround them, take-home pay increases instantly. The only deduction that would remain on our pay stub would be state and local taxes. Yes, I mentioned Social Security. And you'll see by the rest of the plan in this book, that shifting a majority of human services to state and local levels will significantly increase efficiencies. Given the mobility of modern America, states could enjoy honest competition for business, jobs and growth without federal dollars skewing the system.

3. A national sales tax would stimulate savings and level the playing field for all income groups. By eliminating all the corporate loopholes and deductions, we can take class warfare discussions off the tax debate table. There would be no more cries of "tax deals for the rich." Those arguments wouldn't exist anymore. No more loopholes. None. A consumption tax is fair and it creates a *bonus* revenue source: underground income. That is revenue that is never reported by the millions of illegal aliens working for CASH as well as all the drug lords and Mafiosos who deal only in

CASH. When we tax consumption, even underground cash income, (which the government currently has no ability to tax and no way to quantify), is added to the pool. So, if you are an illegal immigrant, you'll pay taxes. If you are a drug dealer, same deal.

Think this is a small change? According to economists Edgar L. Fiege and Richard Cebula, unreported income is $1.8–$2.4 trillion, most of which is reinvested into the marketplace. There is a minimum bonus to the government of $200–$300 billion that could fund half of Medicare or defense, without 4,450 CPAs and 88,000 hours of tax compliance mumbo jumbo. The answer is a simple 10% "sales" or "VAT" tax on everything sold with the exception of fresh foods and prescription drugs.

That's zero personal income tax for individuals.

How about corporations? Put a 10% flat tax on all corporate profits. No fancy loopholes, no special interest (i.e., unions and big corporation) tax dodges. A corporation has net income and that net income will be taxed at 10%. Period. Yes, that's a simple 10% tax on net income.

The only expenses allowed would be actual expenses used to make and sell its products and services. No depreciation. No "paper losses" and no phantom "tax credits" that the lobbyists get greased to slide through for Wall Street fat cats. When a company nets $100, they pay $10. That's it.

How is it possible to enact these changes? The solution is elegantly simple.

Currently, nearly all consumer goods are purchased from a point of sale (POS) device. Most people still call these "cash registers." In order to switch our federal income tax system from the convoluted and grossly overstaffed multi-billion-dollar debacle, a modest 10% sales tax must be enacted on all goods sold. State and local governments currently operate seamlessly by collecting a significant portion of their revenue through this system (a very simple sales tax). Adding a single new national sales tax line to this system could be designed, implemented and rolled out on a national scale realistically in twelve months. Nearly all POS cash register systems are already set up to program this type of entry with little or no expense.

But what about all that infrastructure?

There are over 100,000 grossly overpaid employees at the IRS. There are IRS offices in every major city. Every federal office not only has employees, benefits, pensions, utilities and office spaces, but they all buy pens, paper, computers and spend a king's ransom on consultants and support services and staff to keep their inefficient operation moving along in the bureaucratic quagmire of paper pushing.

Where would all of those people go? What about all of the tax accountants, attorneys and companies that support our need to decrypt 74,608 pages of tax code?

The average federal employee has a nice, juicy pension. When you let 90% of them go, many will retire. For those who are too young to retire, like any industry that is obsolete, retraining is in order. Same fate for the tax preparers, CPA firms and all the wasteful paper-shuffling subsidiaries that soak up our financial and emotional resources.

We didn't protect the VHS tape manufacturers when DVDs became the better solution, and we didn't protect DVD manufacturers when Netflix and other streaming services came along, so we sure as hell should not keep any institution in business, public or private, just for the sake of giving somebody a job. Remember, in the case of the IRS, those salaries are all coming from our wallets. Our tax dollars are spent collecting our tax dollars.

Take $12 billion of its $13 billion budget and strike it from the deficit column. Then add back in the additional revenue collected from the underground economy, and we are on our way to a simple, yet well-funded lean government.

And that is just one department…

Chapter Five

Education: Local School Boards Don't Meet in D.C.

—∿∿—

"An investment in Knowledge pays the best interest."

—Benjamin Franklin

The original Department of Education was created in 1867. As an agency not represented in the President's Cabinet, (and in response to outcries of government overreach), it quickly became a relatively minor bureau in the Department of the Interior. In 1939, the department was transferred to the Federal Security Agency, where it was renamed the Office of Education. In 1953, the Federal Security Agency was upgraded to cabinet-level status as the Department of Health, Education and Welfare. At that time, before the Department of Education as we know it came along, America was a global leader in math and science. Then, in 1979, President Carter made the Department of Education a Cabinet-level agency.

Comparatively, the United States educational system is more decentralized than many other countries. If you think the bureaucracy is lean, however, forget it. The budget in 2016 was $70.7 billion. This is to run an "oversight" function to your local school board and to ensure your school lunches have the appropriate amount of toxins and red dye #2.

Below is a snapshot of the department heads of this massively inefficient, obsolete and obese department. It doesn't include the bureaucratic minions who are running around and feel it's important that your child isn't being left behind. And keep in mind, this is only one department:

- Office of the Secretary (OS)

- Office of Communications and Outreach (OCO)

- Office of the General Counsel (OGC)

- Office of Inspector General (OIG)

- Office of Legislation and Congressional Affairs (OLCA)

- Office for Civil Rights (OCR)

- Institute of Education Sciences (IES)

- National Center for Education Statistics (NCES)

- National Assessment of Educational Progress (NAEP)

- Education Resources Information Center (ERIC)

- Office of Innovation and Improvement (OII)

- Office of the Chief Financial Officer (OCFO)

- Office of Management (OM)

- Office of the Chief Information Officer (OCIO)

- Office of Planning, Evaluation and Policy Development (OPEPD)

- Risk Management Service (RMS)

- Office of the Under Secretary (OUS)

- Office of Postsecondary Education (OPE)

- Office of Vocational and Adult Education (OVAE)

- Office of Federal Student Aid (FSA)

- President's Advisory Board on Tribal Colleges and Universities

- President's Advisory Board on Historically Black Colleges and Universities

- Office of Elementary and Secondary Education (OESE)

- Office of Migrant Education (OME)

- Student Achievement and School Accountability Programs (SASA)

- President's Advisory Commission on Educational Excellence for Hispanic Americans

- Office of English Language Acquisition (OELA)

- Office of Special Education and Rehabilitative Services (OSERS)

- National Institute on Disability and Rehabilitation Research (NI-DRR)

- Office of Special Education Programs (OSEP)

- Rehabilitation Services Administration (RSA)

- Office of Safe and Drug-Free Schools (OSDFS)

Student achievement and global competitiveness don't seem to have a place.

As of 2015, the United States has been demoted from a global leader in math and science to 30th in math and 19th in science. Why do we need a federal department of education? In high school, I was the student delegate to the student advisory committee of the Illinois State Board of Education, and I'm quite familiar with how that works and what happens. Think of the utter ridiculousness of the following scenario:

First, you pay federal taxes from every paycheck. The largest percentage of your money vaporizes into the salaries, pensions and other frivolities that are too numerous to mention, all benefiting the faceless D.C. bureaucrats. Then the remaining small percentage of your money is returned to your state in programs. But remember, those "programs" come along with countless unfunded mandates, federal guidelines and paperwork just to merely comply with ridiculous regulations and federal mandates, which ends up costing your local school district many times over the original amount granted.

That's a horrible return on investment. We, the American public, should be getting at least two dollars in value back for every dollar invested, no matter what department or program. That's the way the private sector works. We are likely getting a big fat 95% loss on our "investment" and suffering from excessive costs of complying with insane federal mandates and regulations that even the people responsible for regulating them cannot fully understand.

Like most government departments, there are overpaid administrators in place just for the sake of administering other overpaid administrators. No value comes out of that, and we end up with these idiotic programs like "No Child Left Behind," or as I call it, "Make Every Kid a Dumb Ass . . . Especially the Smart Ones."

I know what you are thinking. "Gee, Kent . . . that sounds awfully cynical." I can hear you saying it now. "After all, it's for the children!" Not true.

No Child Left Behind (NCLB), the 8th reauthorization of the Elementary and Secondary Education Act of 1965, is thousands of pages of gobbledygook containing programs that cost taxpayers billions per year. The Office of Management and Budget has estimated that states are burdened annually with 7 million hours of paperwork as a result of NCLB.

After its passage, several states released calculations comparing the administrative cost of compliance with NCLB to the amount of federal money they receive under the law. For example, the Connecticut State Department of Education found out in 2005 that Connecticut received $70.6 million through Title I of NCLB but had to spend $112.2 million in implementation and administrative costs. Not surprisingly, the smart students were effectively being dumbed down so as not to exceed the lazy ones who were being left behind.

How does somebody in a cubicle in Washington know what's good for a kid sitting in my hometown of Gatlinburg, TN? Look at where we are today. How well is the Department of Education working? Let's grade their efforts based on their mission statement. In fact, we'll grade ourselves against the backdrop of that *global competitiveness.*

In 2015, more than 500,000 fifteen-year-old students from 72 countries participated in the following assessment:

2015 PISA AVERAGE SCORES

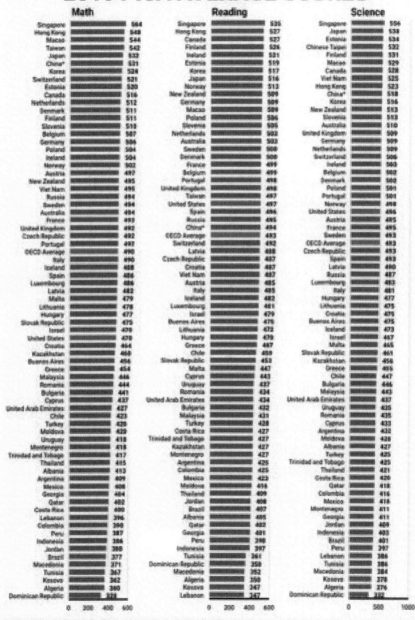

Back in 1997, the United States used to be among the best in the world in math and science. Due in large part to the brain trust running the U.S. Department of Education, we are now behind in math, trailing countries like China, Japan, Austria and twenty-four others. The kids in Taiwan and Macau are better readers than kids in America. I bet the 95% of the kids in the United States not only CAN'T tell you where Taiwan is, they'd probably guess it is a street in China. According to the OECD study on the previous page, the global competitiveness of the students of the United States is not only dead last behind the G7, but in the middle of the pack of countries with the population of Pittsburgh and the innovative acumen of a government union rep.

Many of these countries were Third World nations just a few years ago. They have exploded onto the scene with economies bursting at the seams. And the only thing our kids might even come close to beating them at is Grand Theft Auto. It's probably a good thing, though, because by the time they get out of school, they will have been dumbed down so much that stealing cars may be one of the few employment options they have left.

The folks in these competing countries understand the importance and the value of education. I spend a lot of time in China and Southeast Asia. I speak, meet and interact with these folks regularly. Those kids and their parents are eager to be educated. The overwhelming majority of America's youth today have no appreciation for education nor do they have the motivation to be excited about it. Our nation's youth have fallen victim to the entitlement mentality and don't even realize that, in the future, they are going to have to work to support themselves. The key to their literal survival (barring a rich uncle) is education and motivation—two things that most of America's youth are lacking education and motivation—two things that most of America's youth are lacking.

Education doesn't belong anywhere in the federal government. There's an irresponsible lack of connectivity between our local educational needs and bureaucrats in D.C. They have no clue about the values, cultures and specific needs of our locallocal our communities.

Combine this massive cultural and financial gap with a lack of total accountability to any measurable outcome, and you have a compounded problem. As the gap widens between what is going on in our local schools and the Department of Education, and as test scores continue to plummet, the more the bureaucrats believe that more money, research, resources and energy should be invested at the federal level. The Department of Education sees themselves as the solution. In reality, they are **the *problem.***

At our local level, the elected school board members are our own community leaders made up of our neighbors: farmers, businessmen, workers, teachers, retirees and so on. These are the people who know, love and care about our communities. They understand how our communities work, and they understand what our communities' needs and values are. Let's face it, we are one nation, but we have a variety of cultural and socioeconomic needs across state, county and city lines. Because we do have an array of values and beliefs across our country, nobody knows better how to run its schools than our local school board.

In many school districts, the school board members know every teacher by name, reputation and ability. They know what is working locally and what is not. Many school districts are small enough that everybody knows almost everyone else. Even if the people don't know their school board members personally, they have easy access to them. Local school board members can be held accountable by their constituents, unlike the nameless, faceless bureaucrats loafing in D.C. Do the bureaucrats care about our kids? No. They are likely more concerned about the new fat perk their government workers' union is going to snag for them. Even in the bigger cities, districts are segmented and families who are engaged can have an impact. Parents who are active in their children's lives have a finger on the pulse of their school district's strengths and weaknesses, and if it's not working, they have a voice that can and will be heard.

The federal government, from its cushy, overpriced offices in Washington, has absolutely no way of understanding or effectively "regulating" what's good for my farm-country alma mater in rural, southern Illinois. I promise you that the administrator and his eighteen minions at the National Assessment of Educational Progress don't know Mrs. McGillicuddy, the math teacher at your junior high school, and they certainly don't have a clue on how to increase the test scores in Texarkana, Arkansas or Texas. But I can assure you that the locals fully understand that.

What are we going to do with the Department of Education?

Solution: Eliminate the Department of Education. Period.

In 1996, Bob Dole proposed to eliminate the Department of Education, but he couldn't sell this concept to his colleagues in Congress because the majority of those fellow Congressmen were beholders to the government unions and their bureaucrat members. Can you imagine that? Members of Congress intimated by bureaucrats! The inmates are indeed running the asylum. But Bob Dole was on to something.

Eliminate it! Give the responsibility of educating our children entirely back to our local communities. Seventy percent of your real estate tax bill goes to education. Let's go all-in and restore our desire and ability to educate locally. Let's see how long it takes us to get back to that leadership position in math, science and innovation. We'd see test scores improve and useless compliance issues dissolve away. We would immediately witness a restoration of responsibility and accountability at the local level.

We have nothing to lose. We only have our freedom and future to save. More than that, our country could regain its educational claim to leadership and once again be a place where smart people, innovators and leaders live. The first step is getting the regulatory roadblock of the Department of Education out of the way.

There you go: $69.9 billion saved at the federal level and countless billions saved by local school districts. No one left behind except for thousands of bureaucrats who are responsible for demoting us from being the most educated country in the world to a country that humiliatingly sits currently at 30th, actually trailing some Third World countries.

Forrest Gump may have had it right: "Stupid is as stupid does."

Chapter Six
Welfare: Who Coined the Phrase "Entitlement Program"?

—⚬—

"The most important welfare program in America is a job."

—Newt Gingrich

When we think about welfare, we think of a poor, single mother or an aged person who has no means of support. As an abundant, responsible and caring nation, we have poor people in this country whom we want to help. Until the last few years, the United States has been the richest nation on Earth. How do we have citizens who are sick and dying in our streets without food, shelter and medical care? Shameful! We have to do something. **We are Americans—we can take care of our own.** For years, we did. Unfortunately, the federal government, in its infinite wisdom, screwed it up by placing themselves between us and our ability to take care of our own.

It all started when President Harding proposed a Department of Education and Welfare during his short term (1921-1923), but it wasn't instituted until thirty years later in 1953 when the Department of Health, Education and Welfare (HEW) was established. In 1979, HEW then split up into two separate entities: the Department of Health and Human Services (HHS) and the Department of Education. HHS was in charge of the family support, public health and social security. In 1995, another splintering occurred when the Social Security Administration was removed from HHS and was established as, yet another, independent agency. Great, now we've doubled our chances of success! Under the Obama Administration, the secretaries of HHS were Kathleen Sebelius and Sylvia Matthews Burwell. Kathleen was also the vice-chair of the United States Interagency Council on Homelessness, and HHS is a member of the Council, which is dedicated to *preventing and ending homelessness in America.*

But the truth is, Americans have always taken care of our own citizens. With homeless shelters and local programs available in every major city and many small towns, the only people who are homeless are those who choose to be.

Cruel? Not really.

Mental illness is seen as a contributing factor for many of these people. Our local churches, communities and nonprofits have in the past been able to do a wonderful job helping those who cannot help themselves. This is clearly a case where our local governments and communities are far better equipped to handle a local task with local resources. In addition to shelters, soup kitchens, churches and thousands of nonprofit programs, there are tens of thousands of jobs available for those capable of working, if they ever wanted to work.

A reasonable deal. It's the way our country was founded, after all. Neighbors helping neighbors has always been a cornerstone of our great country. The only problem is that nonprofits are having an increasingly difficult time complying with ridiculous federal government regulations. You see, government regulation for nonprofits is as high (or sometimes even higher) than for for-profit entities. Let's leave it to the bureaucrats to screw it up: "Hmmm . . . What to do . . .

I know! Let's make a regulation to fix this issue! Let's regulate local charities right out of business. Let's make it so difficult to help others that we just walk away from it without helping at all."

Really?

Are donors too ignorant to care about the balance sheet of the nonprofits to which they donate? Not likely. With sites like www. charitynavigator.org ranking in the top 10,000 charity websites on the internet, people are obviously doing their homework before donating their hard-earned money. Do we really need donation police to help us become more careful with our donations? We don't seem to have a problem with people blowing their life savings at a casino. It is incredulous that mountains of paperwork have now been created and must continually be managed to police nonprofits' collection and dispersion of their funds.

In 2012, the New York Council of Nonprofits (NYCON) was troubled by the state government's new legislation on executive compensation. Without question, a nonprofit officer who is responsible for creating a product (philanthropy) and creating revenue (donations) deserves to be compensated. Excessive compensation, however, seems especially distasteful in the nonprofit sector. The proposed New York governor's executive order established an entirely new and unnecessary set of bureaucratic burdens on nonprofits. NYCON noted that multiple state agencies (DOH, OASAS, OMH, OCFS, etc.), were being asked to develop their own separate regulations and procedures which would likely lead to overlapping, conflicting and confusing reporting requirements. "Every new regulation, every new reporting requirement and every new unfunded mandate comes with a cost," said NYCON's Doug Sauer.

He noted that the governor's Task Force on Nonprofit Entities that was appointed to explore the executive compensation issue was already imposing unnecessary compliance costs on nonprofit groups, as well as the state and local governments themselves. The Task Force had reportedly demanded detailed staff salary and compensation data from hundreds of nonprofits with state contracts. But in the Information Age, there is not much information that is secret or hard to come by. "This information already is readily available," said Sauer.

The overregulation of nonprofits has a compounding, detrimental effect. Making nonprofits comply with irrelevant and redundant regulations is a double whammy—not only do they slow down the growth of nonprofits, but they also subsequently hurt the benefactors.

The Department of Health and Human Services (HHS) is the United States government's principal agency for protecting the health of all Americans and providing essential human services, especially for those who are least able to help themselves. As of this writing, the following quote is from the "About Us" page at www.hhs.gov:

"HHS represents almost a quarter of all federal outlays, and it administers more grant dollars than all other federal agencies combined. HHS's Medicare program is the nation's largest health insurer, handling more than 1 billion claims per year. Medicare and Medicaid together provide healthcare insurance for one in four Americans.

HHS works closely with state and local governments, and many HHS-funded services are provided at the local level by state or county agencies, or through private sector grantees. The Department's programs are administered by eleven operating divisions, including eight agencies in the U.S. Public Health Service and three human services agencies. The department includes more than three hundred programs, covering a broad spectrum of activities. In addition to the services they deliver, the HHS programs provide for equitable treatment of beneficiaries nationwide, and they enable the collection of national health and other data."

Really? Keep this in mind: The government can't give you anything they haven't previously taken from you.

At 83,745 employees, HHS is one of the biggest agencies within the U.S. government. Those thousands of bureaucrats occupy over 60,000,000 square feet of prime office space. They have 11 divisions and operate in 1,240 locations in the United States and multiple locations internationally. HHS has a fleet of 795 owned vehicles and 2,930 leased vehicles. Their operating budget for FY 2016 was approximately $83,800,000,000. (By the way, I've read the Constitution numerous times, and I didn't see anything in there about establishing HHS and the federal government having any domain over any area that the HHS covers!)

HHS gloats about how much money it blows on this charade. The bureaucrats are proud of the fact that they have over three hundred separate programs where over 80,000 bureaucrats burn through our dollars in an effort to return to us a tiny percentage of the money it has already taken from us.

One of the agencies within HHS is the United States Public Health Service (PHS) Commissioned Corps, (the uniformed service of the PHS), led by the Surgeon General. This office is responsible for addressing matters concerning public health as authorized by the Secretary or the Assistant Secretary of HHS, in addition to the primary mission of administering the Commissioned Corps.

Another is the Office of Inspector General (OIG-HHS) which investigates criminal activity for HHS. The special agents who work for OIG have the same title Series 1811 training and authority as other federal criminal investigators, such as the FBI, ATF, DEA and the Secret Service. OIG special agents, however, have special skills in investigating white-collar crime related to Medicare and Medicaid fraud and abuse. (Organized crime has dominated the criminal activity relative to this type of fraud for many years. When it comes to investigating this type of crime, the OIG. . . well . . . they suck at it!)

Administering $842 billion in assistance to individual people is the reason the department has a disproportional amount of fraud. This figure accounts for $749 billion or one billion Medicare/Medicaid claims every year! According to James Mehmet, the former chief inspector, up to 40 percent of all claims are questionable. The federal government is woefully unskilled at administering assistance. Medicare and Medicaid account for 70% of HHS's budget. Looking at it, no wonder this national program is ripe for fraud. A state or locally administered program is easier to execute and monitor and could prevent the billions in fraud that occur on a daily basis. The closer a dollar stays to home, the wiser it is managed.

You and I see examples of welfare fraud every day. Can you think of some you've witnessed? Here's one of my favorites from way back: When I was a kid, there was a woman who used to come through the grocery store where I was working. Let's call her Mrs. Smith (not her real name). She was always dressed in really nice clothes, had nice jewelry, and drove a beautiful new car. Each week she would come in and pay for her groceries with food stamps.

One day, I candidly asked her, "Mrs. Smith, may I ask you a question?"

"Yes," she said.

"Why is it that you always wear really nice clothes, have lots of jewelry, have a really nice car, and are using food stamps?"

Apparently, that wasn't the question she was expecting from a fourteen-year-old bag boy at a grocery store. My innocent little inquiry caused the lady to get her undies in quite a wad.

"Nosey little bastard," she grumbled, and she stormed out of the store. Hmm . . . I guess I hit a nerve.

A few hours later the owner of the store called me in to have a little chat. He was certainly not happy that he lost a customer but, to his credit, he also agreed that the lady was defrauding the system. We went on to discuss the fact that her husband also had a very nice car and the latest and best golf clubs, something I already knew because I was also a caddie and worker at the golf course, in addition to my booming lawn mowing business.

Getting your first job is rather interesting. Back in "the day," when I was earning $3.13 per hour, my take-home pay was obviously quite less. All I had to do was look at my pay stub and see where the taxes were going. It was at this moment when I realized a healthy portion of my earnings, meager as they were, were used to pay for those lazy assholes' luxury items.

This is wrong on two levels:

1.) She obviously was defrauding the system. She was married to a guy with a high-paying job and she had the means to live well. But, she saw that the opportunity was there to scheme the system. To me, she was an outright thief. She was stealing the money from my hard-earned paycheck. She may as well have taken that money directly out of my wallet.

2.) In addition to stealing money from you and me, she was stealing money from other people who *truly* needed the assistance.
   If there had been local accountability put in place for this program, the likelihood of fraud would have been much lower.

Do you still think HHS needs to be a federally managed bureaucracy? Let's see what the trustees of Medicare have to say about that. According to their own Summary of 2016 Annual Report:

"The projected seventy-five-year actuarial deficit in the Medicare Trust Fund is up from 0.64 percent from last year's report. The Medicare fund fails the test of short-range financial adequacy, as projected assets drop below one year's projected expenditures early in 2016. The fund also continues to fail the long-range test of close actuarial balance. Medicare's Trust Fund is expected to pay out more in hospital benefits and other expenditures than it receives in income in all future years. The projected date of Trust Fund exhaustion is 2024, five years earlier than estimated in last year's report, at which time dedicated revenues would be sufficient to pay 90 percent of Medicare costs. The share of Medicare expenditures that can be financed with Medicare-dedicated revenues is projected to decline slowly to 75 percent in 2045. Over seventy-five years, Medicare's actuarial imbalance is estimated to be equivalent to 21 percent of tax receipts."

Equivalent to 21% percent of all tax receipts? Say goodbye to your bright future.

Would you trust the guys who projected trust fund exhaustion in 2029 at last year's meeting, and then changed their numbers to 2024 the very next year? If they are five years off on this number, can we not doubt that next year they could be off another five years, or ten?

Why is the federal government sticking its nose in our healthcare in the first place?

The answer is quite obvious: healthcare and big pharma have *our Congress* and bureaucrats in their pockets. They are two of the biggest political donors, and it's all about the money to get them through the next election cycle. But that's a story for another chapter.

The Hijacking of Healthcare

In 1973, the federal government allowed health insurance carriers to transfer from nonprofit to for-profit enterprises. The change came in the form of the Health Maintenance Organization (HMO) Act of 1973, which took its primary source of inspiration from the Kaiser Permanente Health

Care System. This provision encouraged the creation of organizations that would provide managed care by completely "serving" all its members on the capitation basis. The capitation basis mandates that each physician receives a flat fee for each patient visited, regardless of the amount of time he or she spends with said patient. Within a few years, HMOs were seen as a way to "manage" the care of our nation's health.

A physician working under an HMO contract is subject to a review of his or her decisions by the HMO, utilization reviews, gatekeepers and financial incentives. As a result, independent doctors who were trained to focus on the patient found themselves drowning in a sea of paperwork, regulations and bureaucrats whose job is to withhold care and diagnose patients based on "standardized" rules from the insurance carrier. Managed care has turned into a race for the lowest possible medical loss ratio and the highest profit. The race for profit results in lower quality care, as evidenced by the special cases of HMOs. Providing the least possible care at the highest possible profit margin makes the profit in capitation.

Many physicians will agree that for every dollar invested in your healthcare, over 70% of that dollar goes to regulatory and collection hoops they have to jump through as mandated by the government, managed care companies, insurance carriers and other regulatory bodies too numerous to mention. The overregulation of healthcare, of course, is all about money for big corporations. But for us, it hits home.

Below are three cases resulting from a system that has mutated from the good ol' days when doctors truly cared for their patients to what can only be described today as the irresponsible greed of the healthcare lobby and all it serves. These are some real-world consequences when you put the government and insurance companies in charge of our healthcare:

1. When a couple's daughter was born three months premature, an eye exam indicated she had the early stages of retinopathy, a condition that can be corrected. Doctors assured the parents that there was no cause for alarm and a follow-up test was scheduled. The parents' HMO demanded that they again see a primary care doctor before the test could be approved. That led to an eight-week delay, which resulted in the little girl becoming permanently blind.

2. A healthy two-year-old boy was taken to a local hospital after a fall, with a stick lodged between his upper lip and gums. Once there, healthcare personnel repeatedly misdiagnosed the boy's condition and, mindful of the HMO's cost-consciousness, refused to authorize an $800 CT scan that would have confirmed that he was developing a brain abscess. As a result of this poor treatment, the boy was left blind and brain damaged.

3. A mother in Atlanta called her HMO at 3:30 a.m. to report that her six-month-old boy had a fever of 104°F and was panting and limp. The hotline nurse told the woman to take her child to the HMO's network hospital forty-two miles away, bypassing several closer hospitals. By the time the baby reached the hospital, he was in cardiac arrest and had already suffered severe damage to his limbs from an acute and often fatal disease, meningococcemia. Both his hands and legs had to be amputated. A court subsequently found the HMO at fault.

Patient care and the mission of the medical profession have changed forever. Historically, the physician was independent of the cost issues associated with the patient care that he or she recommended. When we were sick and needed a check-up, we went to our doctor, who would take care of our needs based on symptoms and our individual patient histories, not on the historical average of people in your "category." Professional physicians have always had a close link with the poor of their communities, and they worked under a set of ethics that prohibited patient care from being influenced by anything other than the good of the individual patient. Society supported the physician due to these altruistic ideals and refrained from interference. Prior to the "fix" of HMOs, managed care and greedy insurance companies, our doctors focused on making us better. There was honest competition, and people could afford it.

With out-of-control costs for patients and conflicting demands between patient care and bottom-line survival for doctors, the accelerating demise of healthcare still has an additional catalyst that is driving the health of the nation into the ground—literally. Six feet under, in some cases.

That catalyst is fear. Fear for our lives.

Prior to the 1970s, insurance was "affordable," for lack of a better word. Even before that, before the turn of the century, insurance wasn't even in existence. People were responsible. Why is it that people feel the need to load up on health insurance? Because they are horrified by the high cost of treatment. Why is our healthcare many times higher than the rest of the world? Let's discuss.

My business allows me to travel internationally on a regular basis. Americans who don't travel abroad never get to see what's really happening with the other 7 billion people with whom we share the planet. Many Americans believe the rest of the world to be less medically advanced than America. If I told you that my dentist had a staff of twenty, the most advanced dental equipment available, a Stradivarius in the lobby display case, and was a graduate of Northwestern University's dental school, you'd probably think I would be paying top dollar for my dental care, right?

Wrong.

You see, my dentist did go to Northwestern and he does have a Stradivarius violin in the display case in his lobby (he's a real classical music buff), and his office and staff are second to none. The services and facilities surpass any dental office you would find in Beverly Hills.

But, I pay about 80% less than you do and I get way better dental care. My dentist lives and works in Thailand. Bangkok, to be precise. A city of over 8 million, whose middle class is more aware of healthcare than most populated cities in the world. Am I crazy? I don't think so.

An estimated 900,000 Americans went abroad for healthcare in 2013, and an estimated 1.4 million sought healthcare outside the United States in 2016. This 35% increase of people leaving the country for better and more affordable healthcare is showing no signs of slowing down. Once again, increases in regulation, paperwork and government intervention for "the common good" is creating a downward spiral for American healthcare. The less amount doctors earn, the more our brightest minds seek careers outside of medicine.

Isn't it our *right* to be able to get treated for illness? No. It's not.

Healthcare is an earned privilege and a responsibility, but *not* a right. Should we take care of those in need? Of course. And we did until the insurance companies and attorneys got involved, making it almost impossible for a local doctor or hospital to treat those in need. Healthcare has somehow morphed from an earned privilege into a right. Government officials and the lobbyists have burned into our subconscious that the government owes us healthcare, even though it isn't anywhere in our Constitution nor was ever meant to be.

Our healthcare system is another misnomer, anyway. Big pharmaceuticals jokingly call it "disease maintenance," because nearly all the money spent on healthcare goes to managing diseases. Studies prove that 90% of those diseases can be prevented with proper diet and exercise. Period. If we truly wanted to "cure" cancer or eradicate disease in this country, we would plow our resources into prevention instead of treatment. Preventing illness, of course, would eventually put the pharmaceutical companies and their morally bankrupt lobbyists at risk of not hitting the growth numbers that Wall Street demands of them.

In order to keep that parasitic industry alive, they need to keep funding medical colleges so they can continue teaching our doctors-in-training how to prescribe pharmaceuticals and to make a case for questionable surgery and unnecessary testing to become the preferred options over teaching people to walk instead of using the escalator. With obesity pushing 60% of our population and trillions of dollars spent on processed fast foods with no discernible nutritional value, is it any wonder Americans are sick? Our society has become sedentary. The "normal" person today is hunched over, 20–40 pounds overweight, and horribly out of shape.

Where is the "healthcare?"

Caring for disease costs many times more than prevention and promoting a healthy lifestyle. But, nearly all of our hospitals, research facilities, institutes of education and corporations have a vested interest in keeping us sick and diseased. That's where big money is.

Lest you think this is a partial, conservative-based book masked in the title of being focused on the Common Sense 80%, here are some facts and opinions on "disease care":

- The United States has the largest and most profitable pharmaceutical industry in the world.

- Since PDUFA (Prescription Drug User Fee Act) was passed in 1992, pharma companies have paid $7.67 billion to the FDA in application and user fees.

- Since 2016, the pharmaceutical research and development expenditure has been maintaining an increase.

In 2008, impacted by the global financial crisis, the pharmaceutical R & D expenditure totaled $39.2 billion but rebounded to $45.7 billion in 2010.

- There are 2,900 drugs currently in research in the United States, among which 750 are anti-cancer drugs, 312 are for heart diseases, 150 are diabetes drugs, and 109 are AIDS drugs.

(I wonder how much is being invested in broccoli research or the benefits of walking instead of driving six blocks to load up on a Big Mac and fries at the neighborhood McDonald's. I'm guessing $0, of course.)

Follow the money. There is no monetary benefit to the fat cat medical, pharma and insurance lobbies to teach people the benefits of eating healthy, exercising and cutting back on alcohol and drugs. In fact, there is no financial incentive to cure cancer. Nearly all the 750 "anti-cancer" drugs are for treatment. By treating the symptoms and disease, the drug companies can continue to grow and prosper. If and when cancer is finally cured, Pfizer, GlaxoSmithKline and Merck profits will dry up.

Solution: Eliminate the HHS.

With estimates of over half of the $749 billion being squandered by fraud, mismanagement and outright theft, only a swift and dramatic dismantling can end this bleeding.

Why not reform it? Again, that's the fox guarding the henhouse. The only logical solution is to wipe the slate clean and put clear, actionable accountability measures in place. Unfortunately, since lawmakers have a distinct habit of changing their laws, we must remove their power to do what is right for the country.

Here's the Common Sense 80% plan:

1) Eliminate the Department of Health and Human Services.

2) Let the States run, manage, administer and fund the medical care of its poor as they see fit.

The federal government can't give you anything that they haven't previously taken from you. With Medicare, that amount is $7.85 trillion. That's right. Since 1966, when the first Medicare tax was collected, the U.S. government has collected almost $13.9 trillion in revenue that is "supposed" to go into a fund just for Medicare. All of that $749 billion has come from our wallets, minus that same amount attributed to debt. This equals approximately $9,500 per household per year. By eliminating the federal program, 100% of those funds will be the responsibility of you and your local, more-easily-managed government.

Medicare is bankrupt, and we are fueling the system by ignoring preventative healthcare and focusing 30–50% of the money we don't have on the last six months of life in a hospital or nursing home.

There you go. At least another $30 billion saved and probably much more, as most states are required to have a balanced budget. With that control in place, they have a good incentive to be accountable for their spending along with the health of the state's citizens.

Chapter Seven

The Social Security Ponzi Scheme:
Show Me the Money

—∿—

"The real sin with Social Security is that it's a long-term rip-off and a short-term scam."

—Tony Snow

Social Security. Every politician in recent times has lamented the discrepancies in accounting, lauded the purpose, reassured the aged of solvency and promised to overhaul what has indeed become the largest Ponzi scheme in history. They have all avoided leading the nation out of the mess we are in. Now is not the time to blame Bush, Obama or even its creator, FDR— now is the time to fix it! First, let's take a look at how we ended up here.

In 1935, President Franklin D. Roosevelt initially signed Social Security into law as part of his New Deal. At the time, the term *Social Security* covered unemployment insurance as well, something which I apparently must have missed during my many readings of the Constitution. The term, in everyday speech, is used to refer only to the benefits for retirement, disability, survivorship and death—the four main benefits provided by traditional private-sector pension plans.

By dollars paid, the U.S. Social Security program is the largest government program in the world and the single greatest "expenditure" in the federal budget, with 20.8% for Social Security, compared to 20.5% for discretionary defense and 20.1% for Medicare/Medicaid. Social Security is currently the largest social "insurance" program in the United States which, in combined spending for all social insurance programs, constituted 37% of government expenditure and 7% of America's gross domestic product. Social Security is currently estimated to keep roughly 40% of all Americans age sixty-five or older out of poverty (Source: Wikipedia).

When we pay into Social Security, the government calls it a "trust fund." NOTE: There is no "trust fund." The trust fund has taken in $8.7 trillion of your money since its inception, but it doesn't exist. The original logic behind Social Security was a government-sponsored savings plan. But there are no savings. Recipients are being paid from current workers' deposits. It's not even a *hidden* Ponzi scheme. You put a dollar in and, when you retire, get back 70% of it, minus the effects of inflation and lack of interest that could be earned on your money if you had invested it privately. Wow! What a deal!!! It's a huge loss on my investment. Where do I sign up? Oh . . . wait, the federal government already did it for me. Thanks, Uncle Sam!

If you want a snapshot of how utterly ridiculous this system is, you could have spotted it with the first ever monthly recipient of Social Security. The first monthly payment was issued on January 31, 1940, to Ida May Fuller of Ludlow, Vermont. In 1937, 1938, and 1939, she paid a total of $24.75 into the Social Security System. Her first check was for $22.54. After her second check, Fuller already had received more than she contributed over the three-year period. She lived to be 100 and collected a total of $22,888.92.

Did we miscalculate this thing? Pass me the slide ruler, Franklin. Let me see, according to population growth, multiplied by X . . . Uh oh.

The 2016 annual report by the program's Board of Trustees noted the following: In 2016, there were 61 million beneficiaries and 139 million workers paying in. In 2023, total income and interest earned on assets are projected to no longer cover expenditures for Social Security, as demographic shifts overwhelm the scheme. By 2035, the ratio of potential retirees to working-age persons will be 37%—there will be less than three potential income earners for every retiree in the population. The "trust fund" (which doesn't even exist) will be exhausted by 2036 at the latest. (Translation: The federal government analogy would be the tipping point where Bernie Madoff didn't take in enough new investor money to pay off his old investors.)

These are the facts and, given the thousands of dollars you have paid in over the years, you are likely to get an ulcer or feel the urge to go on a mind-numbing drinking binge.

FDR and his staff didn't set off to be post-Depression Madoffs, of course. During the era, 25% unemployment and poverty were common. Social Security began with the best of motives. But, as the saying goes, *"The road to Hell is paved with good intentions."*

In fact, had the government simply left it alone, and let these deductions build up for the people who put their money in, it would be solvent. They'd only be getting back a return of .00000002% minus inflation, still a dreadful loss to us, but they would at least have active forced retirement savings in place.

Instead, the system has been abused, neglected and mutated to the point where, not only does it scarcely resemble the original system, the tinkering of Social Security without any consequences has become the business model for Medicare.

As an investment for you and me, Social Security likely yields a whopping negative return on investment of approximately 50% loss, not counting interest and growth that could have been made had the money been conservatively or privately invested.

For example, in the early 1980s, under the Social Security laws as they existed at that time, several thousand employees of Galveston County, Texas, were allowed to opt out of the Social Security program and have their money placed in a private retirement plan instead. While employees who earned $50,000 per year would have collected

$1,302 per month in Social Security benefits, the private plan paid them $6,843 per month. While employees who earned $20,000 per year would have collected $775 per month in Social Security benefits, the private plan paid them $2,740 per month, at interest rates prevailing in 1996. It also kept the money circulating in the economy, fully void of the government's ability to "borrow it." That's just one massive example of us being able to manage our money better than the federal bureaucrats and our detached elected officials in Washington. Sixty or seventy years ago, when people retired, they retired with a meager pension and a little bit of Social Security. Things are different now. With IRAs, 401(k)s and a hugely abundant economy, despite the cyclical recessions, there are people that have made less than $35,000 a year and have retired with a couple million dollars. That's not unusual for most middle-class baby boomers.

Our economy and investments have outstripped the cost of living and inflation for over 66 years. For those who have put a bit away into any number of savings and retirement accounts, our Social Security package is the smallest percentage of our "retirement" and, for all practical purposes, insignificant.

It doesn't matter if you work for one or 21 different companies during your career, if you're maxing out your retirement accounts, even if you are earning a modest $50,000 a year—at the end of 35 years, unless you have just been absolutely stupid, you've amassed several million dollars!

This wasn't the case years ago, and that's why Social Security was created: to make sure that people had enough to live on after they had retired. The root of the problem is a lack of accountability and the government being allowed to "borrow" our piggy bank. The government decided that the "trust fund" was too juicy a piggy bank to simply leave it alone. They raided it, and IOUs were put in its place. In the private sector, there are "kill switches" in place to prevent what the government has done. At the least, we punish those who abuse it. Let's take the 2011 case of Stephen Dillon of Managed Care Network in Youngstown, New York. Mr. Dillon was charged with and pleaded guilty to embezzling funds from an employee pension fund. As the administrator of the 401(k) pension plan, the defendant was responsible for deducting employee payroll contributions on a biweekly basis. However, Dillon failed to forward those contributions to the plan on behalf of the employees. The penalty is five years in prison, a $250,000 fine, or both. Every private company in America will face the consequences when they misappropriate retirement funds. In many cases, corporate boards and executive teams have been held criminally liable for "borrowing" from their company's retirement or pension fund.

However, it doesn't count when you are the federal government. They don't have the same rules or threshold of proving theft that you and I do. It is not an exaggeration, and it's not an accounting issue. It is actual theft, plain and simple.

Think of it this way. The federal government is the company. You and I are the shareholders. We elect a board of directors (the Congress and the President) to manage our business (the federal government). The officers and board of directors have a fiduciary duty to you, and they are to be held accountable for their actions. Therein lies the rub. No one is being held accountable! The Social Security "trust fund" is the pension plan and it has not been treated like the savings plan it was intended to be. They just know that they have to keep money going into their bloated, out-of-control Ponzi scheme to keep the bureaucratic charade rolling. What our representatives have done is no different than the case of the aforementioned Mr. Dillon. Money has been misappropriated, shifted and outright stolen.

How about a higher profile example? Let's take the largest private embezzlement and compare it to "Social Security." Remember Bernie Madoff? Madoff is a former American businessman, investment advisor and financier. He is the former non-executive chairman of the NASDAQ stock market and the admitted operator of a Ponzi scheme that is considered to be the largest financial fraud in U.S. history—besides Social Security, of course.

In March, 2009, Madoff pleaded guilty to eleven federal felonies and admitted to turning his wealth management business into a massive Ponzi scheme that defrauded thousands of investors of billions of dollars. Madoff said he began the Ponzi scheme in the early 1990s. The amount missing from client accounts, including fabricated gains, was almost $65 billion. The court-appointed trustee estimated actual losses to investors to be $18 billion. On June 29, 2009, Madoff was sentenced to 150 years in prison, the maximum allowed.

Eighteen billion dollars: that's a pretty bloated number, even for the beneficiaries of the interest on all that dough like JP Morgan Chase. Let's compare apples to apples. What is the difference in numbers and actions between Bernie Madoff and the legislators and bureaucrats responsible for our Social Security "trust fund?"

Remember that the concept was a savings account. Put money away for a rainy day, i.e., retirement.

According to the Social Security Administration's website, www.ssa.gov, money going out exceeds money coming in—to the tune of about $5,707,000 per hour! I repeat, PER HOUR. With a $49 billion annual deficit, every hour that ticks by, they are paying out $5.7 million per hour, or about $137 million every single day. In fact, the current unfunded obligation for both Medicare and Social Security is estimated to be over $100 trillion.

Despite this vast obligation, as of 2016, there was only $679 billion in all the Medicare trust funds and only $911 billion in all Social Security funds. To put that in perspective, all the money that we have set aside for future obligations is about one-third of what the federal government spends in one year.

Knowing this, get a recent pay stub and replace the word "FICA" with "Money that has been blatantly stolen from you to maintain a sophisticated Ponzi scheme with absolutely no accountability, and for which you will never have anything to show." While that title may not fit in the same space as "FICA," it is undoubtedly more accurate.

How does that make you feel?

If you think "reform" is in order or there is an accounting method or any "tweak" to fix this boondoggle, get out your calculator, redo the math, and sit your kids down for the sobering news: the money's gone, and if Grandma and Grandpa didn't save responsibly . . . they are coming to live with you—forever.

Here is the summary of the 2016 annual reports from the Social Security and Medicare Boards of Trustees ("Trustees?" Really?!):

Social Security

"When taken in combination, Social Security's retirement and disability trust fund reserves are projected to be exhausted in 2034, the same year that was projected in last year's Trustees Report. After trust fund depletion, annual revenues from the dedicated payroll tax and taxation of Social Security benefits will be sufficient to fund about three-quarters of scheduled benefits through 2090. The 75-year actuarial deficit for the combined trust funds is estimated at 2.66 percent of taxable payroll, down from 2.68 percent of taxable payroll estimated in last year's Report. This improvement reflects a 0.06 percentage point worsening due to extending the projection period and valuation date one year, and a 0.08 percentage point improvement due to new data and improved projection methods."

Medicare

"The Medicare Hospital Insurance (HI) Trust Fund will have sufficient funds to cover its obligations until 2028, two years earlier than projected last year, but still 11 years later than was projected in the last report issued prior to passage of the Affordable Care Act. The projected portion of scheduled benefits that can be financed with dedicated revenues is 87 percent in 2028, declines slowly to 79 percent in 2043, and then gradually increases to 86 percent in 2090. The 75-year actuarial deficit in the HI Trust Fund is projected at 0.73 percent of taxable payroll, up from 0.68 percent projected in last year's report. This improvement reflects a 0.01 percentage point worsening due to extending the projection period and valuation date one year, and a 0.04 percentage point worsening primarily due to higher projected utilization rates, especially in the near term."

Solution: Shut It Down and Give Us Our Money Back Plus Interest.

Most Americans aged 40–50, don't even place their Social Security benefits into their retirement planning. They realistically realize it isn't solvent and likely won't be around. This fact is reflective of the retirement fund landscape for more than two decades.

IRAs have been one of the fastest growing components of the U.S retirement market during the past decade. According to the most recent data from the Investment Company Institute, the total U.S. retirement assets hit $24.9 trillion at the end of March, 2016, up 1.3% from the end of 2015. All told, retirement assets account for 36% of household financial assets in the country. Total assets are more than double what they were in 2000, and up from $18 trillion in 2007.

Shut Social Security down. There is no other option. Our back is against the financial wall of trillion-dollar deficits, and no amount of reform or accounting legerdemain can rescue it.

Phase the closing down of Social Security? Sure. We should set a reasonable timeframe of a few years to shut it down, giving those who can do something time to act on their behalf. More importantly, we can train everyone else to begin to abandon hope of saving this nightmare Ponzi scheme.

A clear and common-sense solution must involve the premise that the government has to refund or credit us for every nickel it has ever taken and hasn't been paid to us. It would have to pay back what it has removed from the fund. Over a two-year phase-out cycle, we could:

1. Pay off all current beneficiaries who have paid in plus interest. Where will they get the money, you ask? The government has plenty of assets. Frankly, I don't care if they have to sell the White House or put Mitch McConnell and Nancy Pelosi out on the street to sell their saggy asses one trick at a time to make restitution. Find the money. Pay it back to its rightful owners (US!). Restitution made. The end. The worst-case scenario, as the United States government liquidates assets to fund the repayment, is to issue tax-free interest-bearing bonds (IOUs) to all of us for the full amount owed plus interest from day one. It's simple, and we would at least know that we will eventually get our money. An IOU

backed by "The Full Faith of the United States Government!" Granted, it doesn't sound too appealing given the actual financial condition of the government, but at least we know where we stand and we can hold the IOU or government bond as an interest-bearing asset.

2. Alternatively, if states wanted to set up a retirement fund, perhaps they could place the money in an *actual* fund and use it through the local banks to fund privately managed, low-risk, mid-yield mortgage funds that could be used to responsibly finance homes for qualified buyers (the old-fashioned way with good credit and a 20% down payment). Leave no room for Madoff-style stealing or Barney Frank-induced Freddie Mac or Fannie Mae lobbyist maneuvering that led our country into the 2008 financial crisis.

Read the comparison between Madoff and Social Security a second time. Now, look in the mirror and ask yourself, "What can I do about it?"

To quote the character Howard Beale in the 1976 classic film Network, we should be saying: "I'm mad as hell, and I'm not going to take it anymore!"

There is no exaggeration when I say our current crop of bought-and-paid-for "public servants" are absolutely out of control and are ruining our country. Social Security is just an example. To simply put our heads in the sand and ignore the facts won't make them go away. That is why Trump was elected and why "establishment" members of Congress are being ousted in record numbers.

Chapter Eight
Subsidies, Grants and Other
Stupid Frat Boy Pranks

—ɯ—

"Every time you cut programs, you take away a person who has a vested interest in high taxes, and you put him on the tax rolls and make him a taxpayer. A farmer on subsidies is part welfare bum, whereas a free-market farmer is a small businessman with a gun."

— **Grover Norquist**

In the previous chapter, we covered the origins of the Department of Health and Human Services (HHS). With their massive Medicare and Medicaid budgets and likely pilfering of nearly $300 billion per year from fraud and corruption, we left out the 441 grants, loans and subsidy programs that HHS and five other departments dole out annually. In a stroke of genius, the federal government has, at least, consolidated their giveaway grants and assistance programs in a catalog. Hey, if Sears can do it, why not Uncle Sam? Managed by the General Services Administration (GSA), this catalog of treasure can be viewed for free at www.cfda.gov. On this site, you can apply for grants, loans, subsidies or any assistance imaginable (and even more that are unimaginable, which is a nice way of saying, "un-freakin-believable!"). The Catalog of Federal Domestic Assistance (CDFA) Programs contains detailed descriptions for 2,203 federal assistance programs. There are five major departments that have established "assistance" programs for our country. That is government-speak for taking your money, wasting 90% on administration costs, and giving the leftover change to people and companies who, for the most part don't need it and, in many cases, acquire it fraudulently. In the past few years, poor underprivileged companies were fortunate enough to get away with over $62.4 billion in federal subsidies. Perhaps you've heard of these struggling businesses. They include:

- Boeing

- DuPont

- Exxon Mobil

- FedEx

- General Electric

- IBM

- Verizon

- Wells Fargo

- Bank of America

Not all benefits go to billion-dollar corporations, of course. There are dozens—strike that, there are hundreds—of individual programs that are freely giving away your money including:

- 441 programs at the Department of Health and Human Services

- 255 programs at the Department of the Interior

- 240 programs at the Department of Agriculture

- 151 programs at the Department of Education

- 125 programs at the Department of Justice

The number of programs is teeming with intelligent ways to waste your money. There are over 66 separate groups within these five major departments that are busily taking our money, including:

Name	Programs
Agency for International Development	12
Appalachian Regional Commission	5
Architectural and Transportation Barriers Compliance Board	1
Barry Goldwater Scholarship and Excellence In Education Foundation	1
Broadcasting Board of Governors	1
Christopher Columbus Fellowship Foundation	4
Commodity Futures Trading Commission	1
Corporation for National and Community Service	16
Delta Regional Authority	3
Denali Commission	1
Department of Agriculture	240
Department of Commerce	96
Department of Defense	73
Department of Education	151
Department of Energy	37
Department of Health and Human Services	441

Department of Homeland Security	101
Department of Housing and Urban Development	121
Department of Justice	125
Department of Labor	60
Department of the Interior	254
Department of the Treasury	10
Department of Transportation	82
Department of Veterans Affairs	47
Environmental Protection Agency	108
Equal Employment Opportunity Commission	6
Executive Office of the President	2
Export-Import Bank of the United States	1
Federal Communications Commission	1
Federal Council on the Arts and the Humanities	1
Federal Maritime Commission	1
Federal Mediation and Conciliation Service	2
Federal Trade Commission	1
General Services Administration	4
Government Printing Office	2
Harry S. Truman Scholarship Foundation	1
Institute of Museum and Library Services	11
James Madison Memorial Fellowship Foundation	1
Japan-U.S. Friendship Commission	1
Library of Congress	4
Millennium Challenge Corporation	3
Morris K. Udall Foundation	3
National Aeronautics and Space Administration	11

National Archives and Records Administration	3
National Credit Union Administration	2
National Endowment for the Arts	2
National Endowment for the Humanities	10
National Gallery of Art	1
National Labor Relations Board	1
National Science Foundation	12
Northern Border Regional Commission	0
Nuclear Regulatory Commission	4
Office of Personnel Management	7
Overseas Private Investment Corporation	2
Peace Corps	0
Pension Benefit Guaranty Corporation	1
Railroad Retirement Board	2
Securities and Exchange Commission	1
Small Business Administration	28
Smithsonian Institution	1
Social Security Administration	9
U.S. Commission on Civil Rights	1
U.S. Department of State	60
U.S. Election Assistance Commission	4
United States Institute of Peace	3
Woodrow Wilson International Center for Scholars	1

Glancing at the above list of grants and subsidies is depressing, especially when you see multimillion-dollar grants going to such important causes as Japan-U.S. Friendship Commission. (Can't they just friend us on Facebook?) Or the Architectural and Transportation Barriers Compliance Board.

(What the hell is that, anyway?) Even in the case of subsidies that are meant to "stimulate" or prop up an industry, we have an annual squandering of billions of dollars. It's all a complete waste and should be eliminated because:

A) It is administered by the federal government, the same fellas who buy $700 hammers and $1,200 toilet seats and have zero accountability toward their expenditures and;

B) Because if there is no market for a product, why would you need or want to subsidize it? Protect a job? If that is the philosophy, then we should go back and rescue a few of those horse-drawn coaches and whip makers and help them out. Ah, what the hell, let's go back and protect the entire buggy industry from those evil car manufacturers.

You see, there is absolutely no argument to have a subsidy of any kind. Businesses come and go all the time. Industries fade away and get replaced with better ones. The only thing a subsidy does is artificially skew the natural market and slow down progress. This is price fixing in its most obvious and ugly form.

At least when someone in the private sector illegally fixes prices, someone is making a profit!

I am sure that the Museum Professionals of America appreciate the extra $984,000 of your money they received to increase their training and knowledge on how to give better lectures at the National Museum of Funeral History (and yes, it's real). The fact that there are well-meaning people willing to devote their lives to doling out money we don't have on projects that we don't care about or even need is nauseating and should be relegated to the federally-funded Toilet Museum. Right?

Not only is the federal government spending more money than it takes in on existing programs and nonsense, but it has added more subsidies and grants with an increase of over 110% since 1985. The largest increase has been from 2005 to 2010 with a whopping 356 new federal subsidy programs earmarked, executed and happily spending your money. Thanks to George W., Barack O., and all the myopic legislators who have "always done it this way" because changing the system would cost them their hard-earned campaign contributions from the fat cats on Wall Street, K Street and the labor unions.

Is there a case for subsidizing struggling industries? Don't we have a national interest in seeing our farms continue to prosper when prices plummet?

While we may nod our philosophical heads that it is important to fund a grant or loan on energy research . . . it isn't. It is the energy companies' business to create, develop and market "energy" in whatever form they see fit. When they use their own risk capital, it is the shareholder's capital, and they are made very aware of the risk and rewards of those investments. The company may also use its own retained earnings for research and development if it so chooses. In fact, it can also piss away its profits and equity on whiskey and whores like Enron and Tyco did, and others that have been known to do so on occasion. Whatever the case, it's within the "private sector where research and development flourish."

The marketplace will eventually reward prudent investment and punish irresponsible behavior.

If a company wants to invest in research and development, it will be able to adapt to the changes in the marketplace and technological advances by its competitors. If it chooses not to invest, eventually it will fizzle out and die. Not merely because it was shortsighted or ignorant, but because, like the dinosaurs, it was supposed to die. There is this thing called a 'free market' that works smoothly and fairly and is actually a natural law of the universe. In Michael Rothschild's book Bionomics, he outlines that economics operate very similar to ecosystems. Adaptation is not only a function of biology. The same laws apply to a market-driven economy. That's why it is the fairest system available. It isn't perfect, but it is indeed an absolute equalizer, especially when cronyism and government corruption aren't involved. One thing I know for sure, every business owner and his or her employees agree on this point. Keep the government and their over-reaching restrictive policies out of business and personal lives. As private citizens and shareholders, we are way better stewards of our money than the federal government!

Moreover, all the historical, technological and game-changing breakthroughs are made by individuals and/or companies in the private sector. Isn't that right, Steve Jobs, Bill Gates, Henry Ford, Orville and Wilbur Wright? Hmmm . . . I don't recall seeing Obama's Solyndra on the Forbes list of top stock picks. Oh, that's right. It's gone, along with $500,000,000 of our money that the government wasted funding it through shady federal subsidies.

It is interesting to note from a subsidy and educational perspective that the Wright brothers were a couple of high school dropouts who ran a bicycle shop. They got the crazy idea that they could build a flying machine. The dream of flying was nothing new; it's just that they were living during the Industrial Revolution and had seen all the rapidly developing technology and thought, "Why not?"

At the same time, distinguished and overeducated Professor Samuel P. Langley was working on his own flying machine. With his great international reputation as a "top scientist," he procured funds from the U.S. government to do his experimentations in order to build a flying machine. There were others in the modern world trying to accomplish the same thing, but Langley's reputation made him the overwhelming favorite. Langley got to waste $70,000 of taxpayer money—that is equivalent to over $2 million adjusted for inflation. Like most government-backed boondoggles, his project failed miserably. The Wright brothers spent $1,200 ($24,000 today) of their own money, and they got the job done!

The private sector by its very nature has to operate in reality—not "theory."

So it is with pure, naturally flowing free market and unmanipulated economic systems.

Fiscally responsible farmers, energy producers and technology companies flourish, and the others do not. Just like any business, those that survive are supposed to survive because they are doing it "right."

Foreign Subsidies

With over $20.5 trillion in debt and $109 trillion unfunded liabilities, how can we justify giving money to other countries? If your family was broke and the only way to support them was to borrow money, would you take some of that money and give it to another family *before* you took care of your own?

The few Americans who have taken the time recently to put down their meth pipe and turn their TV from WWE and/or mind-numbing video games know that we, as a country, are deeply and seriously in debt. You'd have to be living under a rock not to know this. Why, then, do so many folks in the U.S. still feel it is acceptable or even expected that our government sends aid to other countries in the form of food, money, military or otherwise?

There are thousands of charities and private enterprises that already do that and do it very efficiently. In fact, many of these same charities would prefer to do more domestic charity, but the regulations and red tape required by local, state and federal lawmakers have made it too complicated to give domestically. These well-meaning organizations find it much easier to donate their time and financial resources abroad. D.C.'s current system of graft, corruption, irresponsible greed and cronyism is so entrenched in our political and economic infrastructure that nobody is brave enough to tear it down and return us to the pure and honorable system Jefferson, Franklin and the Founders created. Our population feels falsely abundant, confident and affluent, even though our country is, in reality, bankrupt.

Not to mention that our children are the most undereducated of all the developed nations. Many people still believe we are the "richest nation on Earth" and that it would be cruel to ignore the starving kids in Ethiopia or the political refugees from Liberia. We think we have the resources to help, assist and spread our wealth and democracy to other nations.

NEWSFLASH: We don't!

Instead, even with a debt load of $20 trillion, we blindly give away billions of dollars we don't have.

And it's getting worse.

In 2009 the U.S. State Department budget for Bilateral Economic Assistance was $22.5 billion. In 2016, that increased over 23% percent to almost $28 billion . . . that's $27.8 billion every year, folks. With $25.8 billion every year going to this one line item (the total state department budget is $54.08 billion), the simple math is, per returns filed, you gave $181 last year to allegedly help people in another country. We use the word "allegedly" because at least half of that $181 went to bureaucratic administrative costs, payoffs and outright ridiculous, wasteful and shameful expenditures.

Is there a common-sense solution to this never-ending abuse of the "maxed-out" credit card of your tax dollars? And, I think we can all agree that for as long as we have those in need here in America, everyone else will need to stand in line.

Solution: Eliminate All Grants & Subsidies.

This is a no-brainer. When you use the "Agreement" litmus test against nearly all these giveaways, their true colors shine through as pork barrel projects or ridiculous incentives that don't benefit the national interest. I'm sure the Wildlife Without Borders–Africa Program isn't a "must have" federal issue!

If you need further encouragement that almost all these projects and the people that run them should simply go away, I encourage you to review the Appendix, where all 2,203 programs are outlined for you. And keep in mind while you are sleeping, your pockets are being picked clean.

A large percentage of these ridiculous programs are brought upon us by the collusion of our lawmakers and lobbyists. Why? Follow the money.

What about something that still appears to be in our national (and global) interest? One could make the argument that introducing gas mileage standards was necessary, along with hundreds of thousands of pages of legislation and billions in tax dollars.

We can easily let a state do that. The market will always follow. If a company develops a vehicle that gets 100 miles per gallon, the market and the states will clamor to get that company to develop and manufacture it within its borders. They will be rewarded for it. Free Market! The United States is already the world leader in innovation.

We may have given up the title of being a leader in manufacturing, but we have always been the leader of innovation, creativity and entertainment. There is no logic in funding these things on the federal level because states need and will fight for the business. They want industry headquartered in their state, along with the jobs and tax revenues that business brings. There is no reason for the federal government to be subsidizing any technology, even military. Centralized (federal government) development of nearly every innovation breeds waste and corruption. Since they own the printing presses, the federal government has never had to be accountable for money or the lack thereof. States have to be accountable for their budgets—every nickel!

When it comes to research and development of technology that will improve our lives and strengthen our country, you don't have to look any further than Silicon Valley, Research Triangle Park in North Carolina, or a bicycle garage in Ohio.

Similarly, the same thing goes when it comes to foreign aid or helping the poor and disadvantaged, both at home and abroad. If you, like me, feel that we should do something to help out the poor, hungry and poverty-stricken people of this Earth, you can do something about it that works.

Embrace capitalism. No, don't just embrace it – run with it! Encourage it! Feed it in its purest form every chance you get.

I am an auctioneer as a hobby and I donate my time to charities across the country. It's not unusual for me to raise hundreds of thousands of dollars in one night at charity events. Through the efforts of loving, giving individuals, we are sending those funds directly to the people who need it with not a single bureaucrat in the middle "administering" it.

Nobel Peace Prize Winner Muhammad Yunus had a dream to end poverty on the planet—to create a poverty-free world. Not by using centralized, government-assisted welfare to keep poor farmers from developing their own farmland by selling them wheat and corn from the United States. His idea, which has flourished, is called micro-lending. Micro-lending, or very small loans given to entrepreneurs, gives everyone an equal chance of starting and growing their own businesses. It's working, and it's not funded by our government.

And, if you, in our sheltered world called America, think that loaning a woman twenty dollars to start her own basket weaving business is merely a drop in the ocean, you'd be wrong. According to an August 25, 2011, article in the *Daily Star*, rural poverty in Bangladesh came down to 33.1% in 2010 from 52.6% a decade ago as a direct result of micro-lending to start a small business.

Common sense dictates we eliminate all subsidies and grants. Our solution to the lobbying dilemma is a little different.

Chapter Nine
Lobbying: K Street—Washington's 24/7 Red Light District

—∿—

"Real lobbying reform must end the practice of lobbyists writing our laws."

— **Marty Meehan** (Chancellor, University of Massachusetts)

Since the 1970s, there has been explosive growth in the lobbying industry, particularly in Washington. In 2010, lobbying expenses in the federal arena were estimated at $3.5 billion, while it had been only

$1.4 billion in 1998. By 2011, one estimate of overall lobbying spending nationally was $30+ billion.

Here are the top lobbying sectors 1998–2017:

Sector	Total
Miscellaneous Business	$7,737,464,165
Health	$7,655,230,739
Finance/Insurance/Real Estate	$7,629,836,032
Communications/Electronics	$6,115,775,513
Energy/Natural Resources	$5,501,955,135

Other	$3,858,871,821
Transportation	$3,809,956,178
Ideology/Single-Issue	$2,446,357,900
Agribusiness	$2,239,277,712
Defense	$2,162,439,117
Construction	$834,429,786
Labor	$743,167,901
Lawyers & Lobbyists	$468,911,126

And here is a look at how much lobbyist spending has increased from 2002 to 2016:

Year	Lobbyist Expenditures
2002	$1.823 Billion
2003	$2.06 Billion
2004	$2.18 Billion
2005	$2.44 Billion
2006	$2.63 Billion
2007	$2.87 Billion
2008	$3.31 Billion
2009	$3.50 Billion
2010	$3.51 Billion
2011	$3.32 Billion
2012	$3.30 Billion

2013	$3.24 Billion
2014	$3.26 Billion
2015	$3.22 Billion
2016	$3.15 Billion

The overall increase in dollars spent influencing our lawmakers has doubled just since 2002. There is no question that the money invested by primarily large corporations, industry trade groups and unions directly influences the voting by our lawmakers. According to Wikipedia, the general consensus is that lobbying works overall in achieving sought-after results for clients, particularly since it has become so prevalent with substantial and growing budgets.

A study by the investment-research firm Strategas, which was cited in the *Economist* and the *Washington Post,* compared the fifty firms that spent the most on lobbying relative to their assets and compared their financial performance against that of the S&P 500 in the stock market. The study concluded that spending on lobbying was a "spectacular investment" yielding "blistering" returns comparable to a high-flying hedge fund, even despite the financial downturn of the past few years.

The key ingredient necessary for making any lobbying effective is always money. There is strong consensus that this is true, particularly among players in the lobbying industry. Lobbyists "educate" our lawmakers and influence them to not only pass bills but write many bills themselves that the lawmakers who sign them sometimes never even read. In case you were under the impression that this book was "conservative" and would be bashing the left, here's your proof that the Common Sense 80% is not only where my heart is, but it's where 80% of the country's heart is, too.

Here are the top ten lobbying firms and the clientele that they serve:

Lobbying Firm	Revenues	Major Clients
Akin, Gump, et al.	$555,885,000	Insurance, oil, casinos, pharma
Patton Boggs, LLP	$525,422,000	Civil servants, securities, utilities
Cassidy & Assoc.	$416,887,100	Colleges, mining, hospitals, energy
Van Scoyoc Assoc.	$401,793,000	Transit, banking, colleges, counties
Williams & Jensen	$296,754,000	Pharma, utilities, oil, cable, securities
Brownstein, Hyatt et al.	$262,822,000	Securities, casinos, insurance, pharma
Holland & Knight	$261,614,544	Casinos, energy, civil servants
Ernst & Young	$247,936,737	Assurance, tax, advisory, strategic growth markets
Podesta Group	$247,370,000	Banking, pharma, utilities, securities
K&L Gates	$179,110,000	Mfg., environment, food, unions

These are just the top ten. There are hundreds more, including household names like Alcalde & Fay that rake in a cool $160 million a year to shape, influence and control our laws.

Those are just the lobbying firms. According to opensecrets.org, during FY 2016, which includes the presidential election, the top spending by groups/ businesses on lobbying were:

Lobbying Client	Total
US Chamber of Commerce	$103,950,000
National Association of Realtors	$64,821,111
Blue Cross/Blue Shield	$25,006,109
American Hospital Association	$22,117,895
Pharmaceutical Research & Manufacturers of America	$19,730,000
American Medical Association	$19,410,000
Boeing Co.	$17,020,000
National Association of Broadcasters	$16,438,000
AT&T Inc.	$16,370,000
Business Roundtable	$15,700,000
Alphabet In	$15,430,000
Comcast Corp.	$14,330,000
Southern Co.	$13,900,000
Dow Chemical	$13,635,982
Lockheed Martin	$13,615,811
NCTA The Internet & Television Association	$13,420,000
FedEx Corp.	$12,541,000
Northrop Grumman	$12,050,000
Exxon Mobile	$1,840,000
Amazon.com	$11,354,000
Insurance	$152,930,996
Business Associations	$143,141,396
Electronics Reg. & Equipment	$119,587,108
Oil & Gas	$119,129,657
Electric Utilities	$114,331,635
Real Estate	$104,357,207

Hospitals/Nursing Homes	$95,221,803
Securities & Investment	$95,215,398
Air Transport	$86,679,002
Telecom Services	$86,058,723
Health Professionals	$85,061,148
Misc. Manufacturing & Distributing	$78,640,413
Health Services/HMOs	$78,463,804
Education	$74,228,805
Defense Aerospace	$74,218,329
Civil Servants/Public Officials	$69,922,010
Automotive	$62,561,402
TV/Movies/Music	$60,224,797
Commercial Banks	$59,877,406

Hmmm . . . nowhere in that list do I see you and me as average American citizens represented.

According to Common Cause (www.commoncause.org), one of the latest and blatant kowtowing to lobbyists by a legislator was Congressman Mike Horner (R-Florida), whose emails reveal a top lobbyist sending him language for a bill that provides a tax break for companies that contribute to a scholarship fund for low-income students. The legislation increased the tax break from 75% to 100% of the corporate income tax liability. The emails also show that Horner asked for "a blow-by-blow breakdown of what was in the bill" so as not to "embarrass yourself or me, but rather properly defend this bill." This "representative" of the people didn't want to take the time to read the bill he was promoting that a big donor lobbyist had prepared for him. This is a very small example of the insane amount of irresponsibility and gray (very dark gray, bordering on charcoal) area of corruption that is accepted as ordinary business dealings by the insulated demigods of Capitol Hill.

If you want a real doozy, you only have to read Jack Abramoff's tell-all book *Capitol Punishment: The Hard Truth About Washington Corruption from America's Most Notorious Lobbyist* (or watch the movie *Casino Jack*, featuring Kevin Spacey). Abramoff and his partner Mike Scanlon are alleged to have engaged in a series of corrupt practices in connection with their lobbying work for various Indian casino gambling tribes. The fees paid to Abramoff and Scanlon for this work are believed to exceed $85 million.

In particular, Abramoff and Scanlon are alleged to have conspired with Washington power broker Grover Norquist and Christian activist Ralph Reed to coordinate lobbying against their own clients and prospective clients with the objective of forcing them to engage Abramoff and Scanlon in lobbying against their own covert operations. Reed was paid to campaign against gambling interests that competed with Abramoff's clients. Norquist served as a go-between by funneling money to Reed. Abramoff and Scanlon shamelessly filtered millions of dollars and other "benefits" to members of Congress in exchange for votes—all, of course, with a wink and a nod.

Today, Jack Abramoff is not only ashamed of his past life as a lobbyist, but he is working tirelessly to reform the system. Jack Abramoff is a friend, a family man, a great American, and one of the people who can make this reform happen. Jack is now one of the good guys.

D.C. is truly an insulated world of "pay to play" politics. With bills being hundreds and, in many cases, thousands of pages long like the tax code, no single lawmaker has read many of them, and fewer still are drafting them.

The lobbyists are increasing their power through their abilities to not only influence our lawmakers based on their knowledge but also on that all-important currency that now controls Washington: money = votes =

power = money = more power for self-serving special interests = "I get to stay in office."

Solution: Starve the Beast.

Step 1: Require all lobbyist meetings of any kind with any government official (elected, appointed and staff) to be held in a public forum, recorded, broadcast and archived for everyone to see. Any member of Congress or staffer meeting privately "off the record" with a lobbyist, even for a drink, is immediately expelled.

Step 2: Similar to education, the IRS, and a host of other D.C. problems, the only surefire method to improve our government is to dismantle the corrupt infrastructure that binds it. When we implement strict term limits, lobbyists will no longer be able to dangle the money-soaked 'I got your voting block here' influence upon our lawmakers. When we strip them of their ability to become re-elected, lawmakers can devote 100% of their efforts to governing as opposed to running never-ending re-election fundraising efforts.

Prior to and during their tenure, however, lobbyists will still be a force to be reckoned with. By imposing VERY strict term limits, we restrict the flow of lobbying money, but don't eliminate it. In order to truly restore honor and fair representation to our lawmakers, they have to knowingly limit their own power. With a reduction in the size and ability to influence in Washington, the lobbyists—and the irresponsible corporate and special interest greed that fuels them—will be castrated.

"Money goes where the herd flows" is a popular saying in marketing, and it is no less true for the multi-trillion-dollar ATM machine that is Washington, D.C. The system is currently entrenched with well-funded lobbyists whose influence not only creates policy but very often writes it. It has to come to an end now!

Big businesses currently have no choice but to fight for their influence in D.C. so long as they have the power to receive government favors and influence legislation that can stifle their competitors and promote regulations that make it almost impossible for small businesses to start up, operate and compete against them. The freer the market is, the less the "puppet master" lobbyists can dictate self-serving policy. As odd as the Occupy Wall Street movement was, they were certainly right in that those big corporations and special interests control the government and it is the lobbyists who do the bidding for them in Washington. The real dirty work is done on K Street, not Wall Street. It's certainly no coincidence that Wall Street gets the direct benefits from K Street.

Lobbying as a citizen isn't necessarily a bad thing. It's an expression of our right to "petition the government for a redress of grievances." It can provide information to politicians. Unfortunately, the current system allows only the wealthiest and most influential lobbyists to have real access to our lawmakers. As politicians have gotten into the habit of handing out favors to those who send money their way, the system has everyone falling into the same blatantly corrupted trap. Even well-intentioned junior statesmen have no protection or insulation powers against the lobbyist juggernaut.

The only way to reduce the power of lobbyists is to reduce the power of government. The ability to make that happen rests with us, the Common Sense 80%. If voters keep electing lifetime politicians and ignoring the Common Sense 80%, then the power of the federal government and influential lobbyists will continue to grow and skew the system away from true representation.

Term limits! One term, to be exact. We'll discuss this in detail a little later in the book.

Chapter Ten
Defense and Other Tales
that Wag Dogs

—⚍—

"National security is the first duty of government but we are also committed to reversing the substantial erosion of civil liberties."

— Theresa May

The United States Congress created the War Department in 1789 and the Navy Department in 1798. The secretaries of each of these departments reported directly to the President as cabinet-level advisors. In a special message to Congress on December 19, 1945, President Harry Truman proposed the creation of a unified department of state defense, citing both wasteful military spending and interdepartmental conflicts. Deliberations in Congress went on for months, focusing heavily on the role of the military in society and the threat of granting too much military power to the executive branch.

On July 26, 1947, Truman signed the National Security Act of 1947, which set up a unified military command known as the "National Military Establishment," as well as the Central Intelligence Agency, the National Security Council, National Security Resources Board, United States Air Force (formerly the Army Air Forces), and the Joint Chiefs of Staff. The act placed the National Military Establishment under the control of a single Secretary of Defense. The National Military Establishment was renamed the Department of Defense (DOD) on August 10, 1949, in an amendment to the original 1947 law.

The U.S. Department of Defense is one of the few departments that is best suited to be established and managed at the federal level. Outside of our federal military branches, our state-run National Guard units are a vital resource for a myriad of services. In a post-9/11 world, however, our intelligence, terror prevention and "big stick" policies have done wonders to prevent conflicts that poorer nations have been unable to thwart. Also, being a nation as large as ours, having two oceans on two sides of our borders, has insulated us from more wars than any other nation in history (being one of the youngest nations has also helped). Regardless, we grew into a superpower after the Industrial Revolution because we have been a country that, until recently, has enjoyed more freedom than most. It is because of this freedom that our commerce blossomed, which attracted immigrants from around the globe at an unprecedented rate.

Wars have been instrumental in ousting tyranny or supporting liberty for hundreds of cultures for thousands of years. Until we truly evolve as a species, our religious, political and geographic differences will continue to spawn conflict. Threats exist. The Nuclear Age has put the brakes on massive global conflicts, but has the advent of atomic weapons reduced wars?

No. Since the end of the Second World War in 1945, there have been over 250 major wars in which over 23 million people have been killed, tens of millions made homeless, and countless millions injured and/ or bereaved. The United States has been involved in many of these conflicts including Korea, Vietnam and dozens of wars in the Middle East. The industrial-military complex has created thousands of innovations and millions of jobs. Why can't we be a nation like Belize or Costa Rica that has no military?

For better or worse, our economy and the security of our nation still hinges on an efficient, technologically-advanced and rapidly-deployable military. In fact, when you get right down to it, the only two significant products and/or services that the U.S. now brings to the world table are a strong military and pop culture (music, films, fashion, etc.), and much of that is now produced overseas. That's right. About the only thing the world looks for nowadays from the United States is military protection and an occasional obscenity-ridden tune from Jay-Z or Lady Gaga. And, of course, free money and foreign aid.

Isn't it about time we stopped lying to ourselves about how great we are . . . and get down to proving it?!

The amount of money poured into our military is substantial. How it has been allocated, though, is deplorable. The common-sense solution to our over-spending of the military is one upon which well over 80% of the population agrees. Before we talk about the solution, let's discuss the problem.

The military of 1947 pales in comparison to what it has become today. The sheer amount of resources spent annually certainly looks like we are always at war, not simply preparing or preventing one. According to the Department of Defense, there is room for wiser spending—lots of room! I particularly like how Trump started questioning defense spending and re-negotiating contracts from day one. Here are a few 'fun facts' that showcase the scope of our military spending:

- DOD 2010 budgetary resources were pegged at $1.2 trillion, of which $994 billion was disbursed. This amounts to roughly $2,100 per U.S. citizen.

- The DOD uses over $2.2 billion of electricity, enough energy to power more than 2.6 million homes.

- The DOD is responsible for 93% of all U.S. government fuel consumption. Consumption is estimated at 52% by the Air Force, 33%

by the Navy and 7% by the Army. (Now we know why those guys have to march so much!)

- In 2010, DOD spending accounted for 45% of global military spending. More than the next seventeen largest militaries . . . combined.

- We are by far the number one spender on defense. The next top countries by total spending are:

Rank	Country	Spending	% of GDP
1	United States	$611.2	3.3%
2	People's Republic of China	$215.7	1.9%
3	Russia	$69.2	5.3%
4	Saudi Arabia	$63.7	10%
5	India	$55.9	2.6%
6	France	$55.7	2.3%
7	United Kingdom	$48.3	1.9%
8	Japan	$46.1	1.0%
9	Germany	$41.1	1.2%
10	South Korea	$36.8	2.7%

Even following the abysmal record of Obama's lack of military savvy, our military is still second to none and does protect our national interests. We have also protected other nations' national interests. In fact, the United States has had a tendency to play the world's policeman when things get violent abroad. However, we've also had a history of being a bit isolationist. We delayed getting involved (by a year or more) in both of the World Wars and didn't get involved in Indochina until France had gotten its ass kicked.

Foreign policy aside, we need to reduce the waste and massive inefficiencies of our military. As citizens, we all believe that we should take whatever action is needed to be sure we always have the best military in the world. We just need to spend **more efficiently.**

Spending more? I'm good with that, provided we are getting a good value for the goods and services provided by the defense contractors. Our own Government Accounting Office (GAO) report of 2016 analyzed DOD spending and found plenty of items that could save us several billion dollars a year. For example:

DOD Healthcare
Expenditures 2010: $49 billion
Expenditures 2012: $52 billion
FY2017 Budget Request: $48.8 billion

The responsibilities and authorities for DOD's Military Health System (MHS) are distributed among several organizations within DOD with no central command authority or single entity accountable for minimizing costs and achieving efficiencies. The Army, the Navy and the Air Force each has its own headquarters and associated support functions, such as information technology, human capital management, financial activities and contracting. Additionally, the three services each have their own appointed surgeon general to oversee their deployable medical forces and operate their own healthcare systems. Under the MHS current command structure, the Office of the Assistant Secretary of Defense for Health Affairs controls the Defense Health Program budget, but this office does not directly supervise the services' medical personnel.

But the cuts are coming! The DOD has already taken steps (as one of the first federal departments in history!) to reduce its overall budget for FY2017.

DOD Budget (Billions)	FY2014 Actual	FY2015 Enactment	FY2016 Actual	FY2017 Request	FY167 Change
Base	496.3	496.1	521.7	516.1	-5.6
OCO*	85.2	64.2	58.6	82.4	23.8
Total Budget	581.5	560.3	580.3	598.5	18.2

(Source: https://www.thebalance.com/u-s-military-budget-components-challenges-growth-3306320)

*OCO – Overseas Contingency Operations (sometimes referred to as "War Funds")

It looks like President Truman's idea of "consolidating" all the armed forces to increase efficiencies hasn't caught up with how our military personnel manages their medical treatment. That's to be expected. But these things take time. Didn't you get the memo? It's only been 65 years. I'm sure they'll get to it eventually.

Solution, Part 1: Consolidate and Adapt to Current Threats.

Hold the defense contractors accountable. We need more military for *less* money.

The Berlin airlift, rebuilding Japan or doing business with China was not merely Good Samaritan exercises in economic freedoms. Turning our enemies into our allies also insulated us from military threats. It makes no sense to attack your customer or supplier.

Barring our state department sticking its nose into conflicts in which we don't belong, the threat of terrorism is the only current military threat we have. In fact, Hawaii and Alaska aside—which were not states during World War II—our shores have never been attacked by a foreign government since the 1846 Mexican-American War. Every single conflict since 1846, except the Civil War, involved America sending our troops to other countries. We've protected our friends, fought tyranny and inflamed Indochina with our fears of communism. But no government has invaded our borders. Those two large oceans have done wonders for our country.

Since it is implausible that any country could possibly attack us, one could assume that our military shouldn't design strategies and deployment for major conflicts. However, Theodore Roosevelt's "speak softly and carry a big stick" policy may be attributed to our relatively clean record of not being invaded by a foreign government.

The military should be run more efficiently. The separate departments of Navy, Air Force, Army and Marines have always squabbled over power and authority. In many cases, deployment, strategy and equipment on these separate departments are required. However, in thousands of other areas where there is no discernible difference between branches, bulk buying and elimination of redundant systems would save billions of dollars. Examples of these areas include supplies, IT, benefits, and outsourced services.

Veterans: this is one area where cost shifting, not cutting, should take place. Any service personnel who have served should not be treated merely as an ordinary citizen. Their benefits should be first class. Specifically, veterans should receive, at a minimum, the same health benefits offered to members of Congress and their high-ranking bureaucratic cronies. People who have spent time in the military have risked life and limb for our freedom, and they deserve the best medical attention available, including—and especially—mental health treatment for those just returning from combat. Period.

(Here's some food for thought: whose idea was it to give members of Congress health benefits which are far superior to those of United States veterans? Most of those Ivy League idiots in Congress never served a day in the military. I'm just saying . . .)

Solution, Part 2: Follow the Three R's - Reduce the Military Research and Development Budget, Restructure Priorities and Revitalize Science.

The overall U.S. defense research and development budget can afford significant reductions even as innovation and transparency are improved. With a clear, comprehensive policy, the hallmarks of a military research effort that has powered the American economy for much of the last century can continue. To make such a change, however, the President and Congress must make the politically difficult decisions that distinguish between military research essentials and wasteful pork, then cut the pork entirely.

Given the country's current financial situation, the overall defense budget must be reduced. These cuts should be realized in the development, demonstration and support areas and in classified programs that, almost by definition, produce little in the way of scientific or technical advances that can be disseminated to the private sector. These overall budget cuts, however, should be combined with a paradigm shift in priorities to address the new security threats we face. In other words, mothball the battleships and build more drones.

Randy Garber and Bob Willen, partners in A. T. Kearney, have outlined a brilliant five-point plan that falls within the Common Sense 80%. In The Hill article from November, 2011, entitled "Restructuring Defense Spending for Today's Budget Reality: Five Principles to Cutting the Defense Budget Without Harming National Security," Garber and Willen state:

"**First,** reduction targets must be broadly known, specific and consistent. The Pentagon worked hard to meet a $450 billion reduction target and now faces the prospects of being asked to "double down" once again. The ensuing cuts should be the last ones—for a long time—so it is important to make the best long-term decisions. Smart reductions align strategy with resources. The nation cannot afford missed shots at a moving target. Continual "starts and stops" across programs drive inefficiencies when the nation can least afford them. Further, the trade-offs made to meet one target might not be optimal for a different target. Guessing if or when the target will change is not only unproductive, but also leads to churn and uncertainty for both the government and the industrial base.

Second, everything must be on the table. Infrastructure, troop levels, benefits, redundant and overlapping organizations, policy enforcement, and similar areas cannot be exempt from consideration. Politics has failed once. Don't make the Pentagon pay twice by constricting the playing field to protect pet political interests. Up-front exemptions prevent full analyses of the appropriate cost, capabilities, and requirements trade-offs.

Third, new delivery models must urgently be entertained and embraced. Real affordability must be achieved, which means generating far greater and faster productivity gains and innovation. Slow, complex and bureaucratic internal decision processes are a formidable impediment to achieving the benefits of productivity gains and innovation. The Pentagon must determine how to buy and adapt innovation to short circuit traditionally slow and costly "special purpose innovation" cycle times. Failure to realize the maximum value per dollar spent translates into program cancellations, volume cuts, and capability erosion. Innovation must be embraced. Nothing less than a zealous focus by all parties on eliminating waste is required.

Fourth, kill the few to save the many. It is better to stop doing a few things entirely than to slow down everything proportionately. Substantial restructuring requires making hard decisions for the long-term. Yes, mandated across-the-board cuts are expedient, but treating everything with equal criticality prevents making smart trade-offs.

Fifth, cutting supplier profits is a short-term solution that creates long-term problems. Trying to fix a $1 trillion hole on the backs of suppliers will fall short of the target, and ultimately result in a "loselose" for industry and the nation's defense capabilities. While pockets of "excess profits" may exist in the U.S. defense industry, government will not make inroads into its budget challenges by reducing suppliers' profit margins. For instance, assume annual (pre-cut) defense expenditures are $400 billion on goods and services, and average supplier profit margins are 10–15 percent. If supplier profit margins are wiped out entirely, the cumulative 10-year savings are $400 to $600 billion. Clearly, this is not a realistic scenario. The budget reductions will already have a big impact on the revenue of defense companies that provide for our nation's defense.

Squeezing supplier profit margins will either lead to supplier exits or underinvestment across the supply base. To take real costs out of the value chain, suppliers must be part of the solution—helping to improve productivity and generate innovation. With the right incentives, total costs can be reduced while sustaining profit margins. Trading cost-based price reductions for higher margins offers a sustainable way to realize higher value per dollar expended.

Just like a corporate board accepts/rejects management plans, so should Congress allow defense leaders to make the appropriate tradeoffs as part of an integrated plan to provide the most capability for the dollars available. The key is to eliminate barriers to transformational change, not erect them.

In corporate restructurings, shareholder value is at stake. In defense restructurings, national security and lives are at stake. The status quo is not an option for the nation's defense. We should settle for nothing less than an urgent and rigorous, fact-based analysis of all options, as suggested in these five guiding principles. The stakes are simply too high to settle for less."

Once again: Spend wisely and get more military for less money!

Chapter Eleven
Campaign Reform and
Marketing Overhaul

—ɯ—

"The 2018 election cycle…is the third consecutive election cycle that the portion of outside spending made up by partially-disclosed groups has more than doubled."

— Anna Massoglia, OpenSecrets.org

In his 1907 State of the Union address, Theodore Roosevelt was dismayed that there were no laws to "hamper an unscrupulous man of unlimited means from buying his way into office." Roosevelt proposed some very radical measures that he hoped would make elections more fair and transparent. To his great embarrassment, Roosevelt was accused of promising a French ambassadorship to a senator from New York in exchange for $200,000 in business campaign donations.

"The need for collecting large campaign funds would vanish if Congress provided an appropriation ample enough to meet the necessity for thorough organization and machinery, which requires a large expenditure of money," Roosevelt stated.

Should campaigns be financed partially or 100% from public funds? Should there be a limit on donations? Doesn't that impede "free speech"?

In 1966, Congress set up the Presidential Election Campaign Fund, financed by an optional check-off box on income tax returns that diverted $1, (which has since been raised to $3), from the U.S. Treasury to a general campaign fund. Candidates were offered large lump sums to cover expenses related to the general election, so long as they agreed not to collect private donations or spend money raised for primary contests. In 1971, Congress passed the Federal Election Campaign Act which required candidates to report expenses and contributions, and consolidated previous efforts to reform campaign finance policy. As Watergate unfolded between 1972 and 1974, which confirmed allegations that Richard Nixon used substantial campaign contributions for illegal purposes, it persuaded Congress to amend public finance laws once again. The new laws sought to limit individual contributions and provide primary candidates with matching funds on small donations.

In every election since that time, candidates taking federal funds for the primary contest agreed to spend a limited amount—set by the FEC—during that stage of the campaign. But candidates must manage their money carefully! Bob Dole reached his spending limit in the 1996 race months before the party's summer convention, leaving him gasping in the final weeks of primaries. This prompted George

W. Bush to opt out of primary public funding altogether in the 2000 election. Bush did take $67.6 million in general election public funds. In 2004, John Kerry and Howard Dean also opted out of primary public funding, with Dean sending an email to supporters asking for their blessing.

After becoming his party's nominee in 2008, Obama declined public financing entirely, and the spending limits that came with it, making him the first major-party candidate since the system was created to reject taxpayers' money for the general election. Now, however, public finance advocates fear that Democratic candidate Barack Obama's decision to change his position and forgo all public funding may signal an end to Roosevelt's apparatus for good. Senator John McCain (R-Arizona) said Obama "has completely reversed himself and gone back, not on his word to me, but the commitment he made to the American people."

Barack Obama's 2008 presidential campaign shattered all records by raising $760 million in that election cycle. That record didn't last long. Obama then raised more than $1 billion for his 2012 re-election campaign. Obama's victory in the general election was aided by his tremendous fundraising success. Since the start of 2007, his campaign relied on big and small donors nearly equally, pulling in successive donations mostly over the internet.

At the time, the 2012 election was the most expensive in history. Presidential candidates raised money in the billion-dollar range, (give or take a couple of million). Then 2016 was a barn burner as well, having $6.8 billion spent according to the Center for Responsive Politics. And that's not counting the millions in the coffers of the parties, political action committees and advocacy groups. A century on, the laws have changed, but the reality hasn't. Running a national election campaign still costs serious amounts of money, and no candidate has ever won a national office on good ideas alone.

In short, while polls show a surge of angry voters pressing Congress to reduce the rampant spending government has been addicted to for decades, lawmakers are spending larger and larger sums every year in order to win favor of special interest contributors through their covert K Street pipelines so that they can secure their own "cushy" government jobs (i.e., re-election). While the lifetime politicians make the rhetorical call for restraint in public spending, there seem to be no limits on what they'll raise and spend to get re-elected. Why should they care? It's not their money, and they need it to get re-elected so they can save us from ourselves.

The problem can only get worse if we examine the total vote power of U.S. companies. U.S. companies have a combined $16.4 trillion in assets. In addition, the total corporate profits in the first quarter of 2017 were $2.11 trillion. That is a lot of money to buy influence.

This issue is not solely contained to presidential election self-serving of interest. Money is pouring into candidates from outside of their districts and states at a record pace. It is estimated that over 50 percent of campaign funding is funneled into Congressional campaigns from outside their district. These special interests from outside your district and state likely have more influence over your Congressmen than you do!

In 2016, overall spending by all candidates was over an astounding $6.8 billion, and $2.65 billion was spent by outside groups such as unions and Super PACs on elections. In 2016, according to OpenSecrets.org, the top twenty organizations for outside campaign funding were:

Rank	Organization	Total	Viewpoint*
1	Fahr LLC	$90,592,095	L
2	Renaissance Technologies	$59,759,207	N
3	Las Vegas Sands	$44,410,302	C
4	Paloma Partners	$41,945,800	L
5	Service Employees International Union	$39,419,103	L
6	Adelson Clinic for Drug Abuse Treatment & Research	$38,847,300	C
7	Newsweb Corp.	$38,793,990	L
8	NextGen Climate Action	$35,454,586	L
9	American Federation of Teachers	$33,639,332	L
10	Priorities USA/ Priorities USA Action	$33,354,790	L
11	National Education Assn	$30,483,062	L
12	Laborers Union	$29,056,974	L
13	Soros Fund Management	$28,765,198	L
14	Elliott Management	$28,063,900	C
15	Carpenters & Joiners Union	$27,284,744	L
16	Bloomberg LP	$24,972,456	L
17	Pritzker Group	$23,996,637	L
18	Uline Inc.	$23,876,072	C
19	Senate Leadership Fund	$22,476,800	C
20	One Nation	$21,700,000	C

*Viewpoint: L = Liberal, C = Conservative, N = On the fence

We are one of the few countries with only two parties. Until the 2016 election, hundreds of millions of dollars going to the Democratic and Republican parties made it nearly impossible for independent candidates of third, fourth or fifth tier parties to have a snowball's chance in hell of being elected—or, for that matter, even getting recognized. In order to get back to a system in which we are all represented equally from within our district, changes need to be made. Now!

As an independent voter and businessman, I am generally against regulation. By and large, regulations inhibit a free market system. But, when regulations are enacted temporarily, they can skew a system to behave properly. After regulations like Affirmative Action (which has completed its mission in America) have run their course, there is no longer a need to keep pushing when the objective has been reached. Election reform, with regulated and fair principles, could also be a temporary adjustment to an ingrained problem.

That's a justified preamble to the solution of putting restrictions on campaign finance.

FYI, I've been involved in and owned media properties and networks, so when I suggest that equal, *free* access be given to all political candidates, I'm suggesting something that hurts my pocketbook in a very direct manner. However, if we don't give access to solid, honorable, new candidates, we won't stem the flood of backroom deals and lobbying money that is gravely influencing elections.

Solution: Level the Field.

In order to drastically reduce the cycle of the influence of the dollar, as opposed to the influence of ideas and people, America needs a major—but very simple—campaign finance overhaul. Here's what needs to happen:

1. Give equal and free access to candidates on public airwaves. Radio, TV and any other public medium would allow the same amount of time for all candidates. Our current system of debates is a good start. The way it is now, when campaigns begin doling out tens of millions of dollars for ads, those who didn't tune into the debate are at the whim of the largest pocketbook of self-serving special interests, not necessarily the candidate with ideas that are in alignment with the voters.

2. Establish a reasonable amount of dollars a candidate can use for campaigning. It shouldn't take millions of dollars to run for Congress. With the establishment of a cap on campaign dollars ($1-2 per resident per district/congressional seat), we level the field.

3. Under no circumstances can a campaign accept money or support from anyone outside his or her representative area (i.e., Congressional district for House members, statewide for Senate members).

4. Shut down Super PACs.

5. Only individuals can donate—not corporations, unions or other special interest groups.

The biggest influence of campaign finance reform, however, is removing incentives for re-election. We send our representatives to D.C. to represent the interests of the people of our district, not to spend the majority of their time raising money for their next election. This brings us to term limits.

Chapter Twelve

Term Limits: "Experience" is Overrated

—◊◊◊—

"Nothing is so essential to the preservation of a Republican government as a periodic rotation."

— George Mason, Founding Father

"Everyone should run for office once in their life, loyally serve their constituents, and then get out before they start to enjoy it."

— Jack Emmons, my father

Just because this chapter is short, it does not mean it lacks importance. In fact, it should be a top priority! If there is one item in the following agreement that can get our government back on track quickly, it is term limits. Strict term limits . . . as in, no opportunity for consecutive re-election. It is indeed time to drain the swamp. Once and for all!

When the states ratified the Constitution between 1787 and 1788, several leading statesmen regarded the lack of mandatory limits to tenure as a dangerous defect, especially with regards to the Presidency and the Senate. Richard Henry Lee viewed the absence of legal limits to tenure as "most highly and dangerously oligarchic." Both Thomas Jefferson and George Mason advised limits on re-election to the Senate and the Presidency.

Mercy Otis Warren, one of America's most prolific writers during the Revolutionary War era, warned that "there is no provision for a rotation, nor any thing to prevent the perpetuity of office in the same hands for life; which by little well timed bribery, will probably be done. . ."

Nostradamus? Hardly. The Founding Fathers were also historians, and they studied the classics well.

Term limits, or *rotation in office,* date back prior to modern history. Both the Spartans and the Athenians in ancient Greece rotated their governing councils once a year. In ancient Rome, elected magistrates served a single term of one year. If they wanted to seek re-election, they had to wait ten years before they could run again. The idea was to frequently rotate authority in order to prevent corruption.

Term limits not only help to keep everyone honest, but it can also keep elected officials in touch with their constituents. George H. W. Bush (Bush Sr.) was a lifetime politician. He was a Vice President, he was a Congressman, and he ran the CIA—he'd been inside Washington forever! It was reported that one day, with cameras running, he went into a grocery store and he saw a barcode on an item he was purchasing. He reportedly said something along the lines of, "*Oh, that's interesting,*" and the cashier at the market had to explain to him what it was. He was so out of touch with us, the American people, having had no idea what a barcode was. This is just one example of how out of touch the establishment is.

Do you know the last time Hillary Clinton had to stand in line at the DMV or spend countless hours sorting through complicated medical bills and insurance claims? I wonder when she last drove a car, let alone waited in traffic like the rest of us. The establishment, up and down the ranks, spend the overwhelming majority of their time in the "D.C. Bubble" and very little time in their states and districts amongst their constituents. They all live a life of entitlement and privilege once they get to D.C.

The original idea of electing members to the House and Senate was set up for statesmen, school teachers, farmers, businessmen and factory workers. Anyone could run for Congress, serve their constituency for a limited period of time, and then go home and go back into their normal life. For years that's what they did. The Congress is elected to serve—not to be served.

Many new politicians start off with good intentions. But when they settle inside the Beltway, they learn quickly that the "D.C. Bubble" culture is powered by lobbying money and gearing up for re-election. As well-intentioned freshman Congressmen file into Washington on their first day, their respective party leaders impart upon them, not the wisdom of our Founding Fathers and how best to serve their constituents, but the method of playing by the rules of PACs and K Street lobbyists, who hold the keys to the kingdom if they want to stay in office. (The keys to the kingdom being the money and influence for their re-election campaign.)

The party leaders also make it clear that if you step out of line, there are dozens of other candidates who can replace you that will gladly play the role of the party's whipping boy in your district. When a Congressman has to focus on maintaining his power because of re-election votes and the self-serving special interests, money gives powers to those votes, and his morality and values almost always take a back seat. And the longer a person is in office, the more immersed he or she becomes in the culture of cronyism. Those who sell their souls to self-serving special interests become entrenched 'Lifers.' The ones who, though well-meaning at first, allowed our country to decline into the mess we are faced with now.

Solution: Term Limits.

Having term limits, especially a system where no consecutive re-election is possible, would dramatically eliminate backdoor lobbying deals and multimillion dollar re-election campaigns. This would immediately demolish the energy and financial resources of the power brokers who push the agenda for self-serving special interest giants in Washington. Without having to continuously worry about re-election, our representatives could give 100% of their focus to the matters at hand and put the needs of their constituents first, knowing that, after their 2-year House term or 6-year Senate term, they will be going back home to live amongst the constituents which they have loyally served. In other words, we could get Jefferson, Franklin, Adams and those good ol' boys back!

Imagine how much better our country would perform if your local school teacher, clergyman, doctor, tradesman or business leader became a member of Congress for one term only. What kind of political climate would we have in Washington if an actual person *of the people* took a few years to serve his or her state and country?

How wonderful would our country be if you—yes you, dear reader— took the document from the back of this book (The Agreement), took a pledge to honor it 100% and ran for office yourself? Or, at the very least, recruited and supported a great candidate?

An army of revolutionary citizens founded this country, and it is up to us to continue the revolutionary momentum our country was built on. When the cause is just, and the values transcend party lines, like the Common Sense 80%, it will work. Edmund Burke said, "The only thing necessary for the triumph of evil is for good men to do nothing." So let's make it happen!

Quite a few years back, I was sitting at a broadcasters' association breakfast with then-Senator Joe Biden. I suggested some of the suggestions now outlined in the "Agreement." Nothing too outrageous, mind you—just things like simplifying the federal government.

He responded, "No, that's not the *way it works*."

And I said, "With all due respect, Senator Biden, did it ever occur to you that the way it works isn't working?"

He nodded in agreement and said, "But it's not quite that easy."

I reminded him that it hasn't worked for a long time and if nothing is changed, nothing will change.

I then went on and asked him for a hair plug doctor referral.

Kidding. But it probably would have been a more substantive conversation!

Joe Biden is a lifer. He has become part of the system that needs to not be modified or reduced, but overhauled completely.

What can you do about it? Can you run for office? Of course!

You don't need a campaign speech, and you don't need to be a slick attorney. All you need is to say, "I'm running on the platform and principles outlined in the 'Agreement.'" If running for office isn't your cup of tea, get behind anyone who agrees with our simple-yet-bold platform of the Common Sense 80%.

In the meantime, while you are contemplating running for office in your state, county, city or Congressional district, ask the current office holder the following questions:

A) Do you think the government is working optimally as it is running right now? (I can tell you for sure, nobody in his or her right mind can answer "Yes" to that question.)

B) Do you love and trust our Constitution enough to sit out after your current term in office, and let someone who hasn't been in your office before have an opportunity to serve?

Joe Biden or any of our lawmakers didn't start off by saying, "I am going to run for office and ruin America." I'm sure that most of them had good intentions; however, the D.C. system they were indoctrinated into is absolutely corrupt and without accountability.

When one asks citizens if they are in favor of term limits, the overwhelming majority (the Common Sense 80%) are strongly in favor of it. Here's what term limits could do for us:

1. Downgrade seniority, favor meritocracy.

2. Build a 'citizen' Congress and drive out career politicians.

3. Totally break ties from special interests and lobbyists.

4. Promote tendencies to vote on principle.

5. Allow elected officials to vote in a way that truly serves their constituency first, not the self-serving special interests that are standing in line to dole out boatloads of cash to fund their re-election.

6. Reduce the power of staff and bureaucracies.

7. Create a natural reduction in wasteful federal spending.

8. Encourage much smaller government.

9. Encourage greater voter participation in elections.

10. Encourage people to serve their country.

I can't imagine a plausible argument not to enact strict term limits immediately. The only one I've ever heard is that once a good person is in office, forcing that person to leave is removing a high-quality leader. This argument can be easily dismissed because it presumes that:

a) There is a finite supply of decent, honorable people who would serve in office. (There isn't. To the contrary, there are *more* good quality candidates than there are positions.)

b) There isn't someone better who could improve the system. (There is . . . it could even be you!)

The bottom line is, under the terms of The Agreement, a person can hold any U.S. Congressional or Senate office for a single term only and must sit out of any elected office for five years before running for another office. And, as a part of The Agreement, they pledge not to lobby or take a government-appointed job for a period of five years after leaving office.

We all win!

The only people who lose are the influence peddlers on K Street and the "lifer" politicians who got us into this mess that we must now find our way out of.

Chapter Thirteen
Order in the Court: Tort Overhaul

—ɷ—

Tort reform also doubles as a fix for the 'Disease Care' crisis.

The U.S. legal system promises that any American who feels they have been injured or victimized is able to seek justice or reparations through the court system. However, the United States has also become the most litigious society in the free world, in part due to major increases in lawsuits involving everything from hot spilled coffee to neighbors' disputes. In fact, Americans spend more on civil litigation than any other industrialized country. Lawsuits, as an industry, eclipse the amount of volume by all U.S. automakers. There are more lawsuits filed than cars made in America!

According to an *Economic Journal* study, we have plenty of incentives and zero risks when becoming the plaintiff in a lawsuit. In most legal systems, the loser in a suit must pay the winner's legal fees. In America, each party is almost always forced to pay its own, no matter how frivolous the claims and/ or outcome. With large payouts for many plaintiffs, many law firms work on contingency and get a big chunk of the money awarded. Simply stated, in the American legal system there's not a lot to risk by filing a lawsuit, no matter the merit. Many of the over 15 million lawsuits filed in the United

States each year are frivolous. The term "frivolous lawsuit" has acquired a broader rhetorical definition in political debates about tort reform, where it is sometimes used by reform advocates to describe legally non-frivolous tort lawsuits that critics believe are without merit, or award high damage awards or settlements relative to actual damages.

Tort reform advocates argue that the present tort system is too expensive, that meritless lawsuits clog up the courts, that per capita tort costs vary significantly from state to state, and that trial attorneys too often receive an overly large percentage of the damages awarded to plaintiffs in tort cases. The typical contingent fee arrangement provides for the lawyer to retain approximately one-third of any recovery. In 2010, the cost was $55.6 billion for medical malpractice, and the average malpractice cost per doctor in 2012 was $23,000 according to one study. A Towers Perrin report indicates that U.S. tort costs were up slightly in 2016, increased significantly in 2017, and shows trends dating back as far as 1950.

According to a 2004 study of medical malpractice costs, "program administration"—defense and underwriting costs—account for approximately 60% of total malpractice costs, and only 50% of total malpractice costs are returned to patients. These costs are high even when compared with other tort-based cases, such as automobile litigation or airplane crashes, that determine fault and compensate victims. Moreover, most patients that receive negligent care never receive any compensation.

The Harvard Medical Practice Study (HMPS) found that only one malpractice claim was filed for every eight negligent medical injuries. Of the legal changes proposed by tort reformers, this study found that states capping payouts and restricting non-economic damages saw an average decrease of 17.1% in malpractice insurance premiums, which is at least a start to bring down the cost of healthcare and allow doctors to practice medicine and not risk management.

It seems logical that the healthcare industry, consumers and the insurance carriers would all want tort reform. With "disease management" costs spiraling out of control, doctors, patients and the companies that have to support big healthcare and insurance corporations are all suffering. If and when we do enact tort reform, who loses?

Should we simply bash those evil, ambulance-chasing attorneys who suckle on the teat of those outrageous $2.7 million lawsuits for spilling coffee in your lap? (By the way, that infamous case was appealed and settled for a paltry $600,000, thankfully.)

Frankly, for that kind of dough, I'd voluntarily soak my private parts in a whistling teakettle at full boil!

Are the trial lawyers the ones who hold the smoking gun of the high cost of healthcare? They clog up our system with hundreds of thousands of frivolous lawsuits every year!

But they have accomplices.

First and foremost, the insurance companies want premiums high because they have a profit margin in all their calculations. The margins they earn make them attractive—very attractive—to investors. Even though they are regulated, the higher the premium, the more profit they earn.

By the way, those investors are the biggest offenders of the influence buying. They are some of the most prominent and self-serving special interests. Buffet, Soros . . . you name it! It's true that Buffet is to be admired for his early investment savvy, but the reality is his D.C. influence buying during the 2009 financial crisis is what allowed him to post record profits. Why else would a guy who was once a young upstart capitalist ever support socialist leaning candidates the likes of Hillary Clinton and Barrack Obama? Sure, he's a capitalist, but he now has the power to buy government influence! Lots of it! Need proof? Look at his sweetheart Bank of America deal a few years back. And the list goes on.

As long as there is profit in suing hospitals, doctors, healthcare and providers, the premium for malpractice and our own health insurance will remain excessive, and the quality of healthcare in the United States will continue to suffer greatly. It was by insurance lobbyists' design that "Obamacare" drove our insurance premiums exponentially higher and the quality of care even further into the ground. When malpractice premiums stay high for the doctors, the doctors have to charge more. Guess what happens to the cost of health insurance? The insurance companies get to charge more so the premiums rise, which means we end up the biggest losers. As it stands now, our ambulance-chasing, lawsuit-happy attorneys are earning millions, and our insurance carriers and the stockholders who feed them are earning billions.

Who is picking up the tab for all these outrageous costs? We are! This problem doesn't exist in most countries. I get my healthcare from one of the top international hospitals in Asia. By not having to be as concerned about frivolous lawsuits, they are able to focus on medicine and provide amazing prevention and treatment.

If you think this problem is political, you are wrong. It is 100% fiscal.

Here are two examples that, if they weren't true, would be hilarious:

1. PETA, the controversial animal-loving organization, held an anti-hunt protest in 2001—defending the rights of deer to live. On the way home from the protest, two members hit a deer which had run on to the highway. The members informed the New Jersey Division of Fish and Wildlife that they intended to sue for damages and injuries. In their letter, they stated that the Division was responsible for the damages "as a result of their deer management program, which includes, in certain circumstances, an affirmative effort to increase deer population." You don't have to be a tree-hugging extremist or a right-wing nut job to recognize that lawsuits like that aren't just wrong, they waste valuable

resources that could go to service issues and victims that are real. Who is responsible for you? You are. Unless you are really stupid . . .

2. In 1999, Daniel Dukes, a twenty-seven-year-old man from Florida, hatched a clever plot so that he could have his lifelong dream of swimming with a whale fulfilled. He hid from the security guards at Sea World and managed to stay in the park after closing. Shortly after, he dived into the tank containing a killer whale—fulfilling his dream. Daniel was killed by the whale. His parents proceeded to sue Sea World because they did not display public warnings that the whale could kill people. They also claimed that the whale was wrongly portrayed as friendly because of the stuffed toys sold there.

Really? I think the warning was in the name "killer whale"! If only frivolous suits like this were uncommon and only featured on privately funded forums such as *Judge Judy!* I am sure that even she would have a few censored comments for the Dukes' legal team.

The simple solution is that the state and federal courts should hold the losing party and their attorneys responsible for their actions. Then we watch as our insurance premiums come down to levels comparable to other countries.

Chapter Fourteen
Criminal Justice: Pay to Play

—⁓—

"Justice without force is powerless; force without justice is tyrannical."

— Blaise Pascal

Justice is a "feel good" term. We want "justice" for what bin Laden did to us. We call for justice when the system takes advantage of a group of people. We use the word "justice" as a method of enforcing moral behavior and solidifying the values of our nation.

What happens when the justice system *itself* is tainted? Do we realize how far down the slippery slope of injustice our country has fallen? The Office of the United States Attorney was created by the Judiciary Act of 1789, along with the Office of Attorney General. The same act also specified the structure of the Supreme Court of the United States and established inferior courts making up the United States Federal Judiciary, including a district court system. Thus, the Office of U.S. Attorney is older than the Department of Justice.

The Judiciary Act of 1789 provided for the appointment in each judicial district a "person learned in the law to act as attorney for the United States . . . whose duty it shall be to prosecute in each district all delinquents for crimes and offenses cognizable under the authority of the United States, and all civil actions in which the United States shall be concerned . . ." Prior to the existence of the Department of Justice, the U.S. Attorneys were independent of the Attorney General and did not come under the AG's supervision and authority until 1870, with the creation of the Department of Justice.

The U.S. Attorney is appointed by the President of the United States for a term of four years, with appointments subject to confirmation by the Senate. A U.S. Attorney shall continue in office, beyond the appointed term, until a successor is appointed and qualified.

It sounds as if these are the good guys. They prosecute hate crimes and investigate civil rights complaints. The Department of Justice (DOJ) investigates human trafficking. Working with the FBI, U.S. Customs and the Drug Enforcement Agency (DEA), federal prosecutors are assigned to cases that are supposed to protect our nation from perpetrators against our national interests. While many of these people are doing a great job, there is an 800-pound gorilla in the room that most citizens haven't a clue about.

Americans have handed, by default, appointed prosecutors an awesome power—the power to destroy fortunes and futures. For every drug dealer they put away, there are honorable businessmen and victims of political vendettas who are being destroyed by the irresponsible power of the DOJ for the sake of achieving more power for themselves and/or silencing an opponent.

And it happens at all levels—county, state and federal.

For example, there was a court-appointed special prosecutor who has now determined severe misconduct in the federal investigation and trial of former Senator, Ted Stevens of Alaska. In August 2008, Stevens was indicted on seven counts of false statement charges for allegedly trying to conceal information on his Senate financial disclosure forms related to a renovation project of his home in Girdwood, Alaska, and other gifts, including a puppy from a charity event, a massage chair and a statue of giant salmon.

After a trial filled with legal gaffes, numerous requests for a mistrial by the defense, and stunning revelations of the prosecutors withholding evidence, Stevens was wrongfully convicted by a federal jury in October 2008, just days before he faced re-election for his Senate seat. Shortly after the trial concluded, a key government witness, David Anderson, came forward and acknowledged that he provided false testimony and that the prosecutors allowed billing records from Anderson to be introduced into evidence even though they knew they were inaccurate.

Is it a coincidence that this all blew up days before he faced re-election for his Senate seat? Not likely.

In the Ted Stevens case, the DOJ had the ability to reallocate national political power. We are seeing a pattern of abuse of this power to influence elections and weed out those bold enough to legitimately challenge authority. The stakes are high and the rules of due process, fair play and ethics simply haven't applied.

Following the trial, Stevens and his longtime former Chief of Staff William "Bill" Phillips were killed in a plane crash in a remote part of Alaska along with the pilot and two others in August 2010. Prosecutor Nicholas Marsh committed suicide in September 2010.

(Wowza! What a convenient coincidence!)

Our federal justice system isn't simply irresponsible. Over the years, some have been corrupted and even criminal. When a prosecutor investigates you, that's the threat of criminal prosecution. And many times, even before charging someone, they leak 'the investigation' to the press in order to torpedo the reputation of their target.

There is a preponderance of cases where people were wrongly accused and, oftentimes, wrongly convicted. The system is no longer founded on seeking the truth. Unfortunately, prosecutors are lauded for earning convictions, whether just or not. People work on incentives, and where those incentives originate is vitally important. With a free market economy, quality products and services are rewarded. When a student studies hard and receives good grades, he or she is afforded more postgraduate opportunities.

In the case of our justice system, prosecutors are rewarded with career advancement and pay based on the number and percentages of convictions. Their "conviction rate" is their status. In effect, they are no different than a used car salesman. They get so many prospects in the door, and they use all their skills and resources to sell every one of them a car. There is no incentive to determine whether the defendant is guilty or not because their reward is, "I convicted the guy" or "I have an 80% conviction rate." That is their currency for career and political advancement. In some cases, it's not simply a matter of advancement; their very livelihood depends on it: "I like my cushy $120,000-a-year job working for Cook County; and if I don't keep my 80% conviction rate up, I'm out the door."

Of course, if the prosecuting body has a really solid case, this goes almost back to tort reform. It's the same analogy. If a prosecutor (county or federal) has a really good case against somebody, then let them bring it on; if they win, fantastic. If they lose, they pay the defendant's defense expenses in full. This will eliminate many bad prosecutions and relieve the system of frivolous, time-wasting and resource-sucking energy. If the result of a faulty prosecution is paying back a couple million bucks in legal fees, a prosecutor will think twice before filing a weak or politically-motivated case.

A friend of mine was one of the heads of the oil and gas department at a large bank in Chicago, back when that bank imploded in the early 1980s. My friend was, and is, truly a great guy who was hugely respected by his peers, clients and even his competitors. Back in the day, during an oil boom when deals were flowing like crude itself, they partied and drank a bit. Regardless, my friend was an honest and moral man, a family man with four young kids and a wife. Federal prosecutors, however, wanted to make an example of someone when the bank folded, so they recklessly indicted three executives, my good friend being one of them. The Feds came at him with all their accusations and unlimited resources. They clearly had no case, yet indicted him on twenty-five charges.

All three men were cleared 100% of any wrongdoing by a jury.

Each of these men had just spent millions of dollars and almost all of their time defending themselves. It took a toll on their reputations, careers and families. And the federal prosecutors were not happy campers. They had just invested millions in a witch hunt that only came up with virtuous businessmen who partied a little too hard. Embarrassed by their failure, they went back and drummed up 20 or so *new* charges on the *same* men.

These gentlemen, who were found innocent of the previous, most egregious 25 charges, were in the pages of the *Wall Street Journal* and the *Chicago Tribune* almost daily when the trial was happening.

When they went to trial on the next twenty charges, the jury again found them totally innocent of all charges. Not surprisingly, they had used up their entire directors' and officers' insurance defense policy. They were indemnified for $6 million in coverage per person and, at that point, it had all been spent. They used what was left of their life savings to finish defending themselves of these bogus, politically-backed, trumped-up charges. By now, they were broke. They were left financially and emotionally broke, with their families and reputations in ruin.

After being cleared twice of over 45 separate charges, the government came back a third time with another 15 different, unsubstantiated charges. Only now these gentlemen didn't have any defense money. The government's case was so weak that they didn't even pressure for a trial. The federal prosecutors more or less said, "We won't take you to trial if you just plead guilty to one charge." With their backs up against the wall, with no manner or means to defend themselves against the unlimited budget and power of federal prosecution, they pled guilty to a single count of mail fraud.

This vicious, malicious and politically-driven vendetta robbed three men of seven years of their life, their savings and, in the case of my dear friend, it cost him his family. The fabric of their lives was shattered. My friend ended up divorced and broke, not simply financially and socially, but as a man who was decimated emotionally. But his children suffered the brunt of it. The government—with over $75 million in prosecutorial resources, from two different jury trials, three rounds of indictments and around 60 separate charges—got one count of mail fraud, and that was only a plea deal just because these guys didn't have the money to fund another defense for themselves.

For the sake of political gain, a federal prosecutor spent $75 million of our money and permanently destroyed three families without batting an eyelash and without any remorse or penalty.

And who says reform is not necessary?

Solution: Loser Pays.

If you are convicted of a crime, you pay the government's cost. If you rob a bank and are convicted, you pay the cost to prosecute you. If you can't earn money in the joint, you pay that debt off as soon as you get out of jail. We can garnish wages for child support, and we can do it for criminals who steal. You get placed on the payment plan whether it's the county, state or Feds.

If you are wrongly accused and are found innocent, the government should pay your expenses. Lest you think this would bankrupt our system, think again.

In this country, court-appointed attorneys represent people all the time. We are already funding those bills. But a loser-pays system would allow an innocent defendant to have resources equal to those of the government and not be limited to a public defender or whatever money he can scrape up to mount a reasonable defense, whether it be for criminal, civil or even tax violations. "Loser pays" is the great equalizer. It takes the big stick away from an already oversized bully. When a person or government entity is accountable for the results they are responsible for, honesty, integrity and fairness will follow. Without foundation for justice, the system and the countless victims of a broken system will continue to suffer.

Chapter Fifteen
Unions Go, Job Opportunities Grow!

—⚏—

"Unions . . . are just a group of highly paid Trotskyites with a grievance."

— Jonathan Simons

Today, unions exist only to extort dues from their many unwilling victims (forced members). The union leaders live high on the hog and use those funds to wield power in D.C. and state houses across our great country. Unions have outlived their purpose and no longer have a reason to exist.

Unions began forming in the mid-nineteenth century. The 1870s and 1880s saw large-scale consolidation. It wasn't until the late nineteenth century, when unions started to band together under a coalition of many national unions, that they became a player in national politics, usually on the side of the Democrats. Rapid growth came in the early twentieth century and, by the mid-1930s, unions had become a permanent factor in industry. The Congress of Industrial Organizations (CIO) split off from the union coalition and competed aggressively for membership. The American Federation of Labor (AFL), however, was always larger. Both unions grew enormously during World War II. But, the Taft-Hartley Act of 1947, a measure that weakened the unions and highly publicized reports of corruption in the Teamsters and other unions, hurt the image of the labor movement during the 1950s. The two major unions merged forces to create the AFL-CIO in 1955.

Unions formed a backbone element of the New Deal coalition and modern liberalism in the United States. The percentage of workers belonging to a union (or "density") in the United States peaked in 1954 at almost 35%. The total number of union members rose in 1979 to an estimated 21 million. Private sector union membership began a steady decline that continues into the 2010s, but the membership of public sector unions grew steadily, now at a whopping 37%.

Another word for unions' labor rates may as well be "price-fixing." Isn't it strange to think someone other than your clients, customers or employer can tell you what your labor is worth? Years ago, when kids were being forced to work in mines and people were being abused and overworked, unions made perfect sense. Those things don't happen anymore. We don't have poor working conditions or slave labor. With an informed society, regulatory controls are less effective. The market and social media are the great equalizers today. A tweet, YouTube video or blog post can influence a company's labor policy faster and more effectively than a union.

Unions have overpriced and under-motivated the American workforce. We used to be a highly productive country. We invented and produced things, shipped them overseas, and sold them to consumers around the world. Many of us remember the perception (and reality) that things made in Japan were cheap and things in the United States were high quality. You read that right. Before World War II, any product stamped "Made in Japan" was largely considered inferior to a U.S.-made product.

(Try telling that to the Detroit auto manufacturers. Hmmm . . . I wonder why it took them so long to figure that out.)

Our labor costs are over several times what the international average is, and our productivity per man hour is less than that of the world average. A U.S. firm can hire a factory in China, pay one-fifth of the labor cost and get approximately four times the productivity. That makes it impossible for

U.S. companies to compete. In short, employers here in the States are getting 10% of the value on their labor dollar compared to those in China, India, Vietnam, the Philippines and Thailand.

Don't believe me? Do you think it is possible to "save" jobs?

Okay, go ahead and require U.S. companies to manufacture here. Let's see who wants to pay $5,000 for their iPhone. Yep, that's right. By the time you factor in nine times the actual start-to-finish labor cost in the United States, you'd be paying about $5,000 for your iPhone, $700 for your Nikes and triple the cost of your automobile.

Real market rates are mutated when a union is involved. When you "buy union" what are you paying for? Does that product have more value? Nope. You are paying for nothing other than a lobbyist's ability to send Congressmen on "fact-finding" tours to Miami and the Dominican Republic, which have included hookers and drugs on occasion. And these are not just fringe benefits, but are almost expected, with a wink and a nod.

In many cases, under total protest, union members are, in effect, paying for unions to retain power—just for the sake of existing. They, in turn, lobby to keep all the insane and outdated labor laws in effect, which drives labor offshore.

The job of any employer is to find and keep the very best and productive talent they can afford to hire. Period. Why would an employer want anything less? Do you think that Ford, GM or Chrysler didn't see the quality, service and value coming from Honda and Toyota in the late '70s and early '80s? Of course they did! Why couldn't they compete? Because they are big, entrenched companies. But is it reasonable to assume it was size alone that prevented them from competing?

Consider companies like Toyota, Nissan and Volkswagen, all of which have manufacturing plants here in America. Their factories here are non-union. The unions have attempted to rally their workers but to no avail. Their employees, who tend to be more educated and better informed than the average laborer, have, in essence, clearly stated, "I'm getting the fatter paycheck. I'm getting better benefits by not having a union involved because I'm not paying extortion money into a union. I'm in a better working environment, and we have a great relationship with management."

Because of a true free-market economy and a mature industry, unions today serve no purpose whatsoever. Today's employers and employees have a much better level of respect for each other, therefore it produces a happy and productive workforce.

Unions, despite their claims of helping the lower and middle class, almost always end up hurting the lower and middle class with their actions. They make it impossible for many people to get jobs. Take Thanksgiving 2012, as an example. The Service Employees International Union (SEIU) led a strike at Los Angeles International Airport. Surely, though, the union members were in solidarity over this, right? Nope. One union member, Frederick McNeil of Aviation Safeguards, was quoted as saying, "We petitioned to leave the SEIU almost a year ago, and the contract ended. And now they're bringing in outsiders to block travelers who are just trying to get home for the holidays. It's ridiculous. People need to understand that SEIU doesn't speak for the employees at Aviation Safeguards."

But that's not how the SEIU leadership saw it. Instead, they felt that management needs to give in on everything because management is ruining everyone's Thanksgiving.

Wait a minute, isn't the SEIU the ones who are striking and disrupting Thanksgiving, just to make a point?

Unions also *keep* people from working. Let's start in Hollywood. The union organization for actors is called the Screen Actors Guild/American

Federation of Television and Radio Artists (SAG-AFTRA). My daughter is a cast member of a top-rated television show that is taped in Los Angeles. She started on

1.(http://www.theblaze.com/stories/2012/11/21/just-in-time-for-thanksgiving-union-strike-aims-to-snarl-lax-traffic/accessed 1/31/13).

the show when she was three years old and is now twelve years old as of this writing. This little girl was forced to join a union because, had she not, she would have been barred from working on the show.

There are television programs, movie productions and other entertainment venues in California (and elsewhere) where great talent would excel. However, if they are not a member of SAG-AFTRA, they can't get hired. That's right, even the actors' unions are keeping people out of work. This also means that many high-quality and important works of art and entertainment aren't getting produced. They are keeping a lot of money out of the economy because unions have artificially inflated the price of talent, and impose their own ridiculous "rules." Unions are counterproductive. They encourage less productivity so that more dues-paying employees are required to fill the workload. Less productivity = more headcount = more dues = more fat living for union leaders. It totally goes against the great work ethic on which our economy was originally founded. The more people get paid on *productivity,* the more money the employer would and could invest to keep them around and grow their business, which means hiring more people. That's simply good business. And a free market always supports productivity. In a manufacturing example, if somebody is exceptionally productive, the factory is going to want to keep him or her. On a television show or in a movie, if somebody is doing well and pulling numbers and making money for the network or studio, the producers will want to keep him or her. Therefore, if a union doesn't protect the guy who is doing a great job, who does the union protect? The union protects slackers. Only.

What specific benefits do unions provide? Do they encourage productivity? Nope. They promote counter-productivity. Union delegations never bargain on productivity, output, morale or the value of the company.

When we disempower the unions, the slackers will go by the wayside. Think of the teachers' unions. They are very influential. There are so many slackers in the teachers' unions that if teachers had to get paid on an incentive basis, (on how their kids tested and how they performed), the slackers would have to either step it up or go away and make room for quality teachers who are truly dedicated to education. There are so many great teachers, and I was fortunate growing up learning from those whom I believe were some of the best. But many of the good ones have become fed up with carrying a heavy workload, so they are retiring early or changing professions altogether.

A few years back, I was the founder and CEO of a national radio network. One day a guy called me up and said, "I'd like to talk to you about becoming an AFTRA union signatory."

I warmly stated, "I don't really have any interest in that." He asked, "What do you mean?"

"I just don't have any interest in that," I said. I had obviously taken him a bit by surprise with my warm, casual yet direct demeanor.

The guy called me back later and said, "If you don't become a union signatory, I could shut you down by barring union members from opening on your shows."

I smiled, and very matter-of-factly said, "Great. When do you want to do that? I have some time this afternoon or tomorrow morning. When would you like to shut me down?"

He stammered a bit and said, "What do you mean?"

I said, "You said you're gonna shut me down, so now would be as good a time as any."

He realized he wasn't going to get anywhere with me or my employees, so he tried a different angle: "One thing I can tell you, you will never have a union guest on your show again."

"Really?" I said. "Why don't you tell them? Because they are the ones calling us wanting to get on-air for publicity. Many of these comedians," (the network was an all-comedy channel, which made this all the more amusing to me), "are out of work because they can't get a union card and many of them aren't meeting their AFTRA minimums, either. So you see, neither one of us are getting any benefit from your union anyway, so why don't you call them up and let them know?" This was too much fun! A few weeks later I called the guy back and said, "Hey, I was wondering, I haven't heard from you in a couple of weeks. You were gonna come and shut me down. Can we go ahead and get that on the schedule, because I've got a tight couple of weeks." I messed with this guy for months, and, like all the unions of today, the guy had nothing to back him up, a total paper tiger.

The solution to almost all these challenges is to open up the market. Specifically, deregulate the labor market, effectively blocking, restricting and eliminating the financial and power incentives that keep broken, bloated and corrupt unions in existence. No new laws needed, just open up the market.

The number of private companies that still employ union labor is on the decline. Market forces have taken hold and, day by day, the United States is, once again, earning a reputation as a quality manufacturer and service provider. U.S.-based Toyota, Nissan and Volkswagen plants are a shining example of non-union labor creating terrific value, and I am proud that we have several of them in my home state of Tennessee.

Public sector unions, however, are not so fortunate. With no accountability in place and no competitive market forces to incentivize productivity, unions have a firm grasp on workforce mentality and the public-sector guidelines that empower them. Public sector unions represent government "workers," folks who have already rightfully earned a reputation for being highly overpaid and massively underproductive. Besides, do cushy, highly-paid, government employees really need a union to protect them from the same government that protects unions?

Go figure!

Solution: Let the Marketplace Work. Top Performers Will Advance and Slackers Will Settle to the Bottom Where They Belong.

Unions are the purest example of dirty money. When we have term limits, fiscal responsibility, a balanced budget, a return to state's rights and a thinner, leaner legislature that creates value, we naturally starve Washington of its addiction to dirty money. A lot of that dirty money comes from unions. By restoring a desire to serve the people instead of collecting power, the flow of dollars, and the union influence behind those dollars, diminishes.

Elimination of government workers in union power will be the natural result of a leaner and more productive federal government. When employers compensate workers based on productivity and service (even in the public sector), the unions will vanish, mainly because their members today are becoming more informed.

By the way, for those deeply entrenched in a union, encourage employees to explore decertification elections. The National Labor Relations Act of 1935 allows employees to call for a special election to completely get rid of the union as their "exclusive representative."

A decertification election will enable employees to revoke the union's certification to be the exclusive bargaining representative. In effect, the union may be voted out of your workplace.

Bye-bye, unions! Hello jobs!

Chapter Sixteen
Affirmative . . . Action?

—⟋⟍—

"My job will be finished when we have a black man

in the White House."

— "Reverend" Jesse Jackson

Affirmative action in the United States began as a tool to address the inequalities for black folks in the 1960s. This specific term was first used to describe U.S. government policy in 1961. Directed to all government contracting agencies, President John F. Kennedy's Executive Order 10925 mandated employers to "take affirmative action to ensure that applicants are employed, and those employees are treated during employment, without regard to their race, creed, color or national origin."

Four years later, President Lyndon B. Johnson pandered to the black community by elaborating on the importance of affirmative action as a gateway to achieving true freedom for blacks. In a commencement speech at Howard University in 1965, President Johnson outlined the basic social science view that supports such policies:

"But nothing in any country touches us more profoundly, and nothing is more freighted with meaning for our own destiny than the revolution of the Negro American.

In far too many ways American Negroes have been another nation: deprived of freedom, crippled by hatred, the doors of opportunity closed to hope.

…But freedom is not enough. You do not wipe away the scars of centuries by saying: Now you are free to go where you want, and do as you desire, and choose the leaders you please.

You do not take a person who, for years, has been hobbled by chains and liberate him, bring him up to the starting line of a race and then say, 'you are free to compete with all the others,' and still justly believe that you have been completely fair.

Wikipedia https://en.wikipedia.org/wiki/Executive_Order_10925

…This is the next and the more profound stage of the battle for civil rights. We seek not just freedom but opportunity. We seek not just legal equity but human ability, not just equality as a right and a theory but equality as a fact and equality as a result

… To this end, equal opportunity is essential, but not enough, not enough."

That's what he said publicly. It's no secret that behind closed doors, LBJ had a propensity to use the infamous "N-word" very liberally. In fact, several close to Johnson claimed he viewed blacks as lesser evolved species. (What a hypocritical asshole.) But, it was evident through his words and actions off-camera that he needed the black vote and would say anything to get it.

As the social science explaining the impact of such 'unseen forces' has developed, affirmative action has widened in scope. In 1967, President Johnson amended a previous executive order on equal employment opportunity to expressly mention "discrimination on account of sex" as well.

One of the United States' first major applications of affirmative action, the Philadelphia Plan, was enacted by the Nixon administration in 1969. The

Revised Philadelphia Plan was controversial for its use of strict quotas and timetables to combat the institutionalized discrimination in the hiring practices of Philadelphia's skilled trade unions.

The concept and application of affirmative action have developed since its inception, though its motivation remains the same. Just as unions had their purpose, and just as we used to have hitching posts for horses, the *reason* we needed affirmative action is no longer prevalent in the United States. Below are eight reasons affirmative action has outlived its usefulness:

1. **Affirmative action leads to reverse discrimination.** Affirmative action is designed to end discrimination and unfair treatment of employees or students based on color, but it does the opposite. Whites who work harder and/or are more qualified can be passed over strictly because they are white. Contrary to many stereotypes, many minorities fall into the middle or upper class, and almost as many whites live in poverty. Unfortunately, the way things are set up now, a poverty-stricken white student who uses discipline and hard work to become the best he can be is consistently passed over for lesser-talented minority students who don't put in as much effort at all.

TeachingAmericanHistory.org

https://teachingamericanhistory.org/library/document/commencement-address-at-howard-universiy-to-fulfill-these-rights/

2. **Affirmative action lowers standards of accountability needed to push students or employees to perform better.** If a minority student can get into a university with a 3.2 grade point average, why should she force herself to get a 4.0? Although most students or employees are truly self-motivated, most people need an extra push or incentive to do their very best. By setting lower standards for admission or hiring, we are lowering the level of accountability. We should reward hard work,

discipline and achievement! We should never reward a student simply because he or she is a certain race or sex, nor punish another student simply because he or she isn't.

3. **Students admitted on this basis are often ill-equipped to handle the schools to which they've been admitted.** Imagine an AA minor league baseball player suddenly asked to bat cleanup in the majors, or a high school science fair contestant suddenly asked to take a job as a rocket scientist at NASA. Sure, there's a possibility of success in these situations, but it's more likely they will be in over their heads. Good schools require high GPA and SAT scores because it is extremely difficult to graduate from them. Thus, when they're forced to lower standards to achieve a minority quota, some students can't keep up. This isn't to say these students are less capable, but the chances are high that, if they can't meet minimum requirements, they probably aren't ready to go there. The much lower graduation rate of minorities is a testament to the fact that they are too often going to schools that don't match their abilities. The original application criteria of schools were put in for a reason. We should adhere to them. No different from rich, white kids whose daddy buys them into a school that is way over their head.

4. **Getting rid of affirmative action would help lead a truly color-blind society.** When you apply for a job or fill out a college application, how often are you asked about things like your hair color, eye color, or height? Unless it's for a modeling or athletic position, probably never. Why? It's because hair color, eye color or height don't have any effect on your ability to do a job or succeed at a school. There's no association between hair/eye color and intelligence, discipline, ambition, character or other essentials. Thus, it's useless to even ask about that information. Conversely, in today's society, there should be no association between skin color and intelligence/discipline/etc. So why do we keep drawing attention to it? Wouldn't it be great if we lived in a society where skin

color was ignored as much as hair and eye color? Stereotypes exist because there is (or was) at least a kernel of truth from its origin. Many people live up to those by living their life in such a way that perpetuates the negative stereotypes. Others are wise enough to rise above their circumstances and succeed. Why are there redneck jokes, black jokes, Asian jokes, and jokes about every other race and religion on the planet? I grew up in the redneck category but was ambitious enough not to live in a double-wide mobile home with junk cars jacked up in the front yard or marry any of my cousins. Ben Carson isn't a thug and Oprah isn't a crack whore. And I am guessing Jack Ma and Yao Ming are excellent drivers. All of us must rise above it!

5. **It is condescending to minorities to say they need affirmative action to succeed.** When you give preferential treatment to minorities in admission or hiring practices, you're in effect saying, "You're not talented enough or capable enough to achieve on your own, so we'll just hand it to you, dumbass." Many of my minority friends find it condescending and insulting to imply that they cannot achieve their goals through hard work and ability.

6. **It demeans true minority achievement. In other words, success is often labeled as a result of affirmative action rather than hard work and ability.** Ask Condi Rice, Colin Powell, Oprah Winfrey, Robert Johnson, Herman Cain or Dr. Ben Carson (who famously called Obama out on his healthcare debacle right in the middle of the presidential prayer breakfast) how they got to where they are. Was it hard work or affirmative action? Everyone achieved their positions through hard work, and because they're bright and articulate. My guess is that they would all be offended if you said they got to where they are because of affirmative action. The same can be said of minority doctors, lawyers, business leaders, etc. Too often, their achievements are demeaned by people who believe preferential treatment got them to their current positions.

7. **Once enacted, affirmative actions are tough to remove, even after the underlying discrimination has been eliminated.** Times change. Societies learn and grow. Racist attitudes dissolve over time, as they have in this country. Even race card extortionists like Al Sharpton, Jesse Jackson and Barack Obama have to admit that racial issues in our country nowadays are worlds ahead of where they were in the '60s. In almost all areas of the country, discrimination and racism are a thing of the past. Still, a number of affirmative action policies remain in place, even when the vast majority of people would agree they're no longer necessary. Unfortunately, lawmakers move slowly and must haggle over everything and pander to everyone. It's tough to get hundreds of people and multiple branches of government to agree on anything. Also, as we all know, the agenda of politicians often don't match those of their constituents. Corruption and special interest groups can influence the government into no action whatsoever. After all, for them, it's all about re-election.

8. **Barack Obama.** Hello? The majority of the country voted a black man into the presidency! The American people, most of whom are white, elected and then re-elected a "black" (well, half-black) president. While our friends across the pond are still killing each other because someone's great-grandfather had a crooked nose, America continues to be the melting pot of cultures and one of the least racist countries on the planet.

Solution: Get Rid of Affirmative Action and Quotas.

If some knucklehead employer wants to discriminate, let him. If there are two candidates for a job and the one with the darker skin is more qualified, and that person is not selected, that's a good thing. Actually, that's a great thing. Here's why:

If some racist idiot doesn't hire a person because of his or her skin color or sex, then that person won't have to put up with their potential boss's bigotry culture. That's better for the employee, and it serves society very well because when that business owner or supervisor tries to compete with another firm who was smart enough to hire the person best suited for the job, the dork with the white sheet will be at a major disadvantage. He will be called out on social media. His business will eventually go broke because he didn't have enough sense to make a great hire. All for the best! If someone is so stupid that they would pass up a great hire because of the color of his or her skin, the hiring manager deserves the failure that awaits him or her, along with a lifetime membership to the Dumbass Hall of Fame.

When the market is free to do its will, it is more colorblind than any of us. Eliminate affirmative action and let the chips fall where they are supposed to. Darwinian economics still work.

Chapter Seventeen
Immigration: Importing
People and Value

—ᴖ—

"A nation that cannot control its borders is not a nation."

— **Ronald Reagan**

We are now living in a world economy. Before the turn of the century, the bulk of our goods came from domestic resources. We imported people in order to handle the burgeoning demand for the production of our products. We imported people and exported goods.

Today, with the proliferation of trade confusion, inequitable tariffs and the lack of a unified immigration policy, our country resembles the proverbial deer in the headlights. Without a congruent plan or an effective means to execute it, we are floundering on all fronts.

I genuinely believe that President Trump is on the right track, but he still has to deal with those in D.C. and beyond who feel the need to pander to people who have made no effort to become legal citizens and who refuse to assimilate into our culture.

Historians estimate that fewer than one million immigrants—perhaps as few as 400,000—crossed the Atlantic Ocean during the seventeenth and eighteenth centuries. Relatively few eighteenth-century immigrants came from England: only 80,000 between 1700 and 1775, compared to 350,000 during the seventeenth century. In addition, between the seventeenth and nineteenth centuries, an estimated 645,000 Africans were brought to what is now the United States.

In the early years of the United States, immigration was fewer than 8,000 people a year. After 1820, immigration gradually increased. From 1850 to 1930, the foreign-born population of the United States increased from 2.2 million to 14.2 million. The highest percentage of foreign-born people in the United States was found in this period, with the peak in 1890 of 14.7%. During this time, the lower costs of oceanic travel made it more advantageous for immigrants to move to the United States than in years prior. From 1880 to 1924, over 25 million Europeans migrated to the United States. Following this period, immigration fell, because Congress passed the Immigration Act of 1924, which favored immigrant source countries that already had many immigrants in the United States by 1890.

The Great Depression dominated immigration patterns of the 1930s and, in the early 1930s, more people exited the United States than immigrated to it. Immigration continued to fall throughout the 1940s and 1950s, but it increased again afterward. After 2000, immigration to the United States numbered approximately one million per year. Despite tougher border security after 9/11, nearly eight million immigrants came to the United States from 2000 to 2005—more than in any other five-year period in the nation's history. More than half entered illegally.

In 2006, 1.27 million immigrants were granted legal residence. Mexico has been the leading source of new U.S. residents for over two decades, with China, India, and the Philippines rounding out the top four.

The United States has often been called the "melting pot," derived from a 1908 play of the same name by Israel Zangwill. This attributed to the

United States' rich tradition of immigrants who came looking for something better by assimilating into American culture and, at the same time, having their cultures melded and incorporated into the fabric of our country.

Appointed by President Clinton, the U.S. Commission on Immigration Reform, led by Barbara Jordan, called for reducing legal immigration to about 550,000 a year. Since 9/11, the politics of immigration has become an extremely hot issue. It was a central topic of the 2008 and 2012 election cycles, then totally exploded in the 2016 election. It is widely believed that the immigration issue is what propelled Donald Trump to a solid victory.

The number of foreign nationals who became legal permanent residents (LPRs) of the United States in 2013 as a result of family reunification (66%) outpaced those who became LPRs on the basis of employment skills (16%) and humanitarian reasons (12%).

Since World War II, more refugees have found homes in the United States than any other nation. Of the top ten countries accepting resettled refugees in 2015, the United States ranked 3rd. The country accepted more than twice as many as the next nine countries *combined*. One econometrics report in 2010, entitled *Immigrant Networks and the U.S. Bilateral Trade: the Role of Immigrant Income* by analyst Kusum Mundra, suggested that immigration positively affected bilateral trade when the United States had a networked community of immigrants, but that the trade benefit was weakened when the immigrants became assimilated into American culture.

That's code for became lazy and figured out how to game the American welfare system.

Wikipedia https://en.wikipedia.org/wiki/Melting_pot

Is immigration a serious threat to our national security? Does the current policy serve our national interests?

Our country has a history of being built almost entirely on immigration. It is not just an essential part of our legacy. The melting pot of culture and values has allowed the cream to rise to the top. We have been the most creative, innovative and, until recently, still one of the freest countries on the planet. We owe a significant amount of our success, then and now, to our immigrants—legal hardworking immigrants. Presently, however, some policy adjustments are necessary. Let's begin with the most visible immigration issue our country has: Mexico.

When I was a kid I mowed yards. That's what I did to make money. A lot of money for a kid. Even as a teenager, I built up a nice savings account mowing yards.

How many kids are mowing yards today? Most American kids have become fat, lazy and are too busy playing Xbox to work or learn how to start a business. What is the reputation of immigrant legal labor? From mechanic shops to beauty salons, business startups by legal immigrants began to outpace U.S.-born business startups in the past decade, according to many reports by New York-based Center for an Urban Future.

"Many legal immigrants come from strong merchant cultures that have existed for centuries," says center director Jonathan Bowles. And they arrive in the United States with a way higher drive and better work ethic than most of today's U.S.-born citizens. In New York City, legal immigrants made up 36% of the population but accounted for 49% of all self-employed workers in 2000, according to the center's report. Legal immigrants drove the growth in the city's self-employed population between 1990 and 2000. The number of legal immigrants who were self-employed jumped 53%, while the number of American-born residents who were self-employed fell 7%.

In Los Angeles, first-generation legal immigrants created at least 22 of the city's 100 fastest growing companies in 2005. Legal immigration and the legal immigrants who start their own businesses have undoubtedly been a significant force in creating jobs and bolstering the U.S. economy.

According to the *Wall Street Journal*, legal immigrants have launched nearly half of America's 50 top venture-funded companies over the last 20 years and are key members of management or product development teams in almost 75% of those companies. These results were published by the National Federation of American Policy (NFAP). This report contained interviews with entrepreneurs who spoke of the appeal of the United States when it came to building businesses.

Dr. Stefan Kraemer, who founded EndoGastric Solutions, legally came to the United States specifically to start a company. He said, "In Germany people would have told me, 'What are you doing? You're a surgeon; why do you want to do anything else, like start a company?' To me, America is about having a dream and being able to realize it." Jeff Graham, the British-born CEO of RGB Networks, echoed Kraemer, "In the rest of the world, when someone presents an idea, the response is often, 'Here's why you can't do it.' In America, the response is, 'Great idea.' That is a unique strength as a nation."

The NFAP says better legislation is needed to keep entrepreneurs and educated workers legally coming to these shores and continuing to build businesses that create jobs and drive the economy. Many legal immigrants are absolutely productive and have come here and built amazing businesses and employ many people.

Wouldn't it be great, like the NFL draft, to be able to trade out a lazy, able-bodied American on welfare for a good, hard-working legal immigrant? In other words, we would trade one hard-working legal immigrant for one of the able-bodied, but lazy Americans who contributes no value to America who continues to rape, pillage and abuse our welfare system at the expense of those who truly need it? Who wouldn't make that trade?

Many Americans have simply become lazy, while many immigrants, legal and illegal, have stepped up and demonstrated hard work, which is exactly what American work ethic and family values used to be. Why not give many of our hardworking immigrant farm workers, landscapers, and laborers, those who have earned it, a path to citizenship? They are way more American than the actual Americans who choose not to be productive.

But, you ask, don't immigrants also take advantage of our welfare system?

Yes, many do. But immigrants are three times more likely to work more than one job, even though we make it difficult for them to start their own business.

"U.S. immigration policy does not look kindly on foreign nationals who seek to create businesses in America," according to a companion report by the NFAP. "In fact, in a practical sense, it may be easier to stay in the United States illegally and start an underground business than to start a business and gain temporary legal status and permanent residence (green card) as the owner of that business."

Solution: Qualified Citizenship.

Maybe it sounds obvious and way too simple, but let's examine what it takes to become a citizen of other countries. Most countries want to see your financials and your record as a citizen, criminal background, affiliations, etc. You'll have to show that you have a job or reliable means of financial support and that you bring enough with you that you won't become a drain on their society. It's that simple. They realize the positive benefit of coming to their country as an asset and not a liability.

This doesn't mean, however, that we should let just anyone into our country. We don't need people immigrating when they don't bring value to our great nation. Just like you and I, we couldn't become a resident of almost any other country unless we can prove that we're bringing value to that country. If I want to retire in Belize or set up residence in emerging countries like Thailand or the Philippines, I have to show my balance sheet, my income statement and my net worth, and jump through numerous hoops to prove that I will bring value to their nation.

If a person from any country brings substantial value to America, has financial and intellectual assets to back it up, let them prove it and let them apply. If they have a job lined up here or are going to start a business that creates jobs well, then, welcome home! We're glad to have you!

The global economy and the market, like the tides of the ocean, always seek a balance in resources, products and commerce. That includes "human resources."

The bottom line on immigration is that the overwhelming majority of immigrants, legal and illegal, are good people. They came here to work and build a better life for their family. On top of that, they share, and in some cases, exemplify and amplify, the values that our great country was built on. They want a better life and better community in which to thrive. That's why so many people are so pro-immigration. Our Common Sense 80% solution gives immigrants an excellent opportunity to come to America, or stay if they are currently undocumented, and it gives the pro-immigration folks a chance to step up and put their money where their mouth is. Granted, some immigrants came here to game our system, while some are outright criminals. Those folks should not only be deported immediately but deported somewhere where they can never come back again—ever.

In the case of the good, honest and hardworking immigrants, they should be allowed to stay under the following conditions:

1. The petitioner and their dependents have ZERO criminal past.

2. They have never EVER taken welfare or public assistance from any government entity in the United States—federal, state or local.

3. The petitioner agrees to never apply for or take welfare and/or public assistance of any kind from any government entity in the United States.

4. The petitioner and dependents are sponsored by two natural-born American citizens who, for a period of ten years, will stand good for and personally guarantee, (with an actual financial guarantee), that the petitioning party and their dependents will not commit a crime, will not apply for or accept any public assistance from any government entity in the United States including federal, state or local and will stand good for all debts incurred and defaulted on by the petitioner. If the petitioner does apply for or accept any such public assistance, the guarantor will be held fully responsible for any and all money accepted and/or court costs incurred and fines or penalties levied upon the petitioner as a result of any crime they commit.

Some of you are saying that these conditions would be too difficult to comply with. I disagree and, in fact, have one undocumented family that I have come to know, love, and trust enough that I would proudly step up and sponsor. So, pro-immigration folks, now is the time for you to put up or shut up.

Chapter Eighteen
National Freedom: Building Our Independence

— ɯ—

"Let's make sure we're doing what we can in our own backyard to gain our energy independence and to create American jobs with American energy."

— **Cory Gardner**

"We have all the resources we need right here in this country to establish energy independence if we had the leadership."

— **Herman Cain**

The U.S. energy situation is a convoluted combination of policies, resources, politics, environment and trade. From the energy standpoint, where we came from may be obvious. Where we are now is worse than you think. But, where we can go is nothing short of miraculous . . . provided we have the intelligence and courage to do what is logical and right.

The 1973 oil crisis made energy a popular topic of discussion in the United States. The U.S. Department of Energy was implemented with the aim of energy conservation and more modern energy producers. It imposed a national maximum speed limit of 55 miles per hour (88 km/h) to help reduce gasoline consumption. Corporate Average Fuel Economy (CAFE) standards were enacted to downsize automobile categories. It imposed a year-round daylight savings time, created the United States Strategic Petroleum Reserve, and introduced the National Energy Act of 1978. Alternate forms of energy and diversified oil supply resulted.

The United States receives approximately 81% of the energy it consumes from fossil fuels such as oil, natural gas and coal. The remaining portion comes primarily from hydroelectric and nuclear stations. Americans constitute less than 5% of the world's population, but consume over 26% of the world's energy to produce 22% of the world's industrial output. We account for about 25% of the world's petroleum consumption, produce only 9% of the world's annual petroleum supply, and have only 3% of the world's known developed oil reserves. We produced 8.9 million barrels of oil daily and produced 749.2 billion cubic meters of natural gas in all of 2016. Meanwhile, we consumed 19.63 million barrels of oil daily and consumed 778.6 billion cubic meters of natural gas in 2016. That means we imported roughly 7.9 billion barrels of oil and 45 billion cubic meters of natural gas in 2016.

Why are we even importing oil and natural gas? The United States is currently sitting on 31 billion barrels of oil and 8.5 trillion cubic meters of natural gas that we know about and have barely begun to scratch the surface.

According to Wikipedia, here are the most recent numbers from the top ten oil producing countries:

Rank	Country/Region	Oil Production (bbl/day)
1	United States	15,043,000
2	Saudi Arabia	12,000,000
3	Russia	10,800,000
4	Iraq	4,451,516
5	Iran	3,990,956
6	China	3,980,650
7	Canada	3,662,694
8	United Arab Emirates	3,106,077
9	Kuwait	2,923,825
10	India	2,515,459

Now, as far as oil consumption goes, here are the numbers from 2017:

Rank	Country/Region	Oil consumption (bbl/day)
1	United States	19,880,000
2	China	13,226,000
3	India	4,990,000
4	Japan	3,988,000
5	Saudi Arabia	3,918,000
6	Russia	3,224,000
7	Brazil	3,017,000
8	South Korea	2,796,000
9	Germany	2,447,000
10	Canada	2,428,000

As of this writing, here are the latest estimates of oil exports, barrels/day:

Rank	Country/Region	Oil exports (bbl/day)
1	Saudi Arabia	8,300,000
2	Russia	5,225,000
3	Iraq	3,800,000
4	United States	3,770,000
5	Canada	3,596,690
6	United Arab Emirates	2,296,473
7	Kuwait	2,050,030
8	Nigeria	1,979,451
9	Qatar	1,477,213
10	Angola	1,420,588

This is the most recent list of countries by crude oil imports, barrels/day:

Rank	Country/Region	Crude oil imports (bbl/day)
1	China	8,400,000
2	United States	7,900,000
3	India	5,123,000
4	Japan	3,441,000
5	South Korea	2,949,000
6	Germany	1,830,000
7	Philippines	1,503,000
8	Italy	1,346,000
9	Spain	1,224,000
10	United Kingdom	1,221,000

This is the 2015 estimates for natural gas exports list:

Rank	Country/Region	Natural gas exports (cu m)
1	Russia	197,700,000,000
2	Qatar	123,900,000,000
3	Norway	112,000,000,000
4	Canada	78,250,000,000
5	Netherlands	53,650,000,000
6	United States	50,520,000,000
7	Algeria	43,420,000,000
8	Turkmenistan	40,300,000,000
9	Malaysia	34,990,000,000
10	Australia	34,060,000,000

These are the latest estimates of natural gas imports:

Rank	Country/Region	Natural gas imports (cu m)
1	Japan	99,774,000,000
2	Germany	99,630,000,000
3	Italy	70,200,000,000
4	United Kingdom	53,630,000,000
5	South Korea	51,888,000,000
6	France	46,200,000,000
7	United States	45,000,000,000
8	Russia	38,200,000,000
9	Turkey	38,040,000,000
10	Spain	36,710,000,000

This table shows the top ten countries based on their oil reserves in 2012 (US ranked #14):

Rank	Country/Region	Total reserves (bbl)
1	Venezuela	296,500,000,000
2	Saudi Arabia	265,400,000,000
3	Canada	175,000,000,000
4	Iran	151,200,000,000
5	Iraq	143,100,000,000
6	Kuwait	101,500,000,000
7	United Arab Emirates	97,800,000,000
8	Russia	80,000,000,000
9	Libya	47,000,000,000
10	Nigeria	37,000,000,000

And, finally, here are the latest numbers on natural gas reserves, from the U.S. Energy Information Administration:

Rank	Country/Region	Proven reserves (bbl)
1	Russia	47,805,000,000
2	Iran	33,721,000,000
3	Qatar	24,072,000,000
4	United States	15,484,000,000
5	Saudi Arabia	8,619,000,000
6	Turkmenistan	7,504,000,000
7	United Arab Emirates	6,091,000,000
8	Venezuela	5,740,000,000
9	Nigeria	5,475,000,000
10	China	5,440,000,000

In the United States, oil is primarily consumed as fuel for cars, buses, trucks and airplanes in the form of gasoline, diesel and jet fuel. Two-thirds of U.S. oil consumption is in the transportation sector. The United States, an important export country for food stocks, converted approximately 26% of its grain output to ethanol in 2016. Across the United States, 40% of the whole corn crop went to ethanol in 2013. The percentage of corn going to biofuel is expected to go up.

Robert Kaufman, an expert on world oil markets and director of Boston University's Center for Energy and Environmental Studies, says, "At its peak in production, which occurred in the 1970s, the United States produced about 10 million barrels of oil a day. Now, after thirty years of fairly steady decline, we produce about 8.9 million barrels a day, whereas we consume 19.63 million barrels daily. Whoever talks about oil independence has to tell a story about how we close about a 15-million-barrel gap."

We used to be an oil exporting country, and now we import the majority of our oil. From whom? The very people who have vowed to bring "Death to America!" ("Marg bar Amrika," as they would say in the Middle East).

In conjunction with our energy policy, usage and imports, we show how we care for the environment. When you compare the United States with every other country, our desire, ability and results of producing energy in an environmentally responsible manner are second to none. The United States leads the world in developing oil in a clean and responsible manner. We excel at it. We, America, are incredible stewards of the Earth's precious environment. On the other hand, look at the leading oil-producing countries such as Saudi Arabia, Iraq, Iran, Venezuela and Mexico.

The priorities for these countries are as follows: "let's produce lots of oil, sell it to the stupid Americans, and then we can use the money they pay us to destroy them." For countries lead by Islamic extremists, making money by selling overpriced oil and using that money, in turn, to terrorize Americans is a great racquet if you are them. However, it sucks for us. Those countries are crack dealers funding our addiction and, with every hit we take from their "crack" oil pipe, we become weaker and weaker, and they become stronger, richer and more powerful.

Consider how clean and responsible we are by what doesn't happen here. Hurricanes are a fact of life, and we have tens of thousands of structures offshore—many in the hurricane zones. However, since oil lines are capped not at the surface, but at or beneath the ocean floor, even if oil platforms snapped loose and blew away, industrial seals restrain potentially destructive petroleum hundreds or even thousands of feet below the waves. Thus, over 3,050 offshore structures endured hurricanes Katrina and Rita in August and September 2005 without environmentally damaging petroleum spills. While 168 platforms and 55 rigs were destroyed or severely damaged, the oil they pumped remained safely entombed, thanks to heavy underwater machinery.

According to the American Petroleum Institute, the oil and gas industry added more than $1.3 trillion to the U.S. economy in 2015, which is about 7% of the nation's gross domestic product. The resources from the Gulf of Mexico account for about 30% of U.S. oil and natural gas production and support more than 170,000 jobs.

According to economist Paul Zane Pilzer, the fuel-injected combustion engine increased the oil "supply." While in the 1970s we believed we only had 40 years of oil left, the people compiling that data assumed our cars would still get ten miles per gallon and that no new technology would stretch the usage of that oil. Below is an excerpt from his book *Unlimited Wealth,* in which he writes:

"For the past four hundred years, virtually all practitioners of the dismal science we call economics have agreed on one basic premise: that a society's wealth is determined by its supply of physical resources. And underlying this premise was that the entire world contains a limited amount of these physical resources. This means, from an economic point of view, that life is what the mathematicians call a zero-sum game. Over the centuries, this view of the world has been responsible for innumerable wars, revolutions, political movements, government policies, business strategies and possibly a religion or two. Once upon a time, it may even have been true.

But not anymore.

Today we do not live in a resource-scarce environment. The businessperson and the politician—as well as the butcher, the baker and the candlestick maker—who continue to behave as if they were operating in the old zero-sum world will soon find themselves eclipsed by those who recognize the new realities and react accordingly.

We live in a world of effectively unlimited resources—a world of unlimited wealth. The ancient alchemists sought to discover the secret of turning base metals into gold; they tried to create great value where little existed before.

If the ancient alchemists had succeeded in fabricating gold, gold would have become worthless, and their efforts would have been for naught. But through their attempts to make gold, they laid the foundation for modern science, which today has accomplished exactly what the alchemists hoped to achieve: the ability to create great value where little existed before. We have achieved this ability through the most common, the most powerful and the most consistently underestimated force in our lives today—technology.

In the alchemic world in which we now live, a society's wealth is still a function of its physical resources, as traditional economics has long maintained. But, unlike the outdated economist, the alchemist of today recognizes that technology controls both the definition and the supply of physical resources. In fact, for the past few decades, it has been the backlog of unimplemented technological advances, rather than unused physical resources, which has been the determinant of real growth."

With technologies such as the fuel-injected engine, directional drilling and environmentally safe tracking, we have effectively created "new supplies" of domestic fuel, making it virtually unlimited. By combining these time-tested techniques in innovative, new ways, we have unlocked a hundred-year supply of cleaner-burning oil and natural gas in the United States.

Similarly, enhanced oil recovery technologies have enabled us to produce energy once believed to be too expensive to recover, allowing us to revitalize mature oil-producing fields thought to be reaching their economic limit.

Legislatively, of course, our bloated government has created countless separate committees, commissions and departments that all have far overreaching environmental authority. While regulation has established standards of environmental responsibility, the duplication and inefficiencies of these departments and people have done a lot of harm as well.

Federal and state responsibility for the preservation of our government has become so fragmented that no member of the administration, Congress or the bureaucrats can interpret it with certainty. The Trump Administration is taking bold steps to correct what they can, but they have a big fight ahead of them, having to deal with multiple layers of territorial bureaucrats and, of course, the lifers in Congress who are funded by those who push for these numerous regulations.

The Environmental Protection Agency (EPA) is the concern of almost two-thirds of the House of Representatives' standing committees and subcommittees, with a similar percentage in the Senate. Some seventy committees and subcommittees control water quality policy, for example. Such fragmentation creates both opportunities and problems. While such a variety of committees provide enormous access for environmentalist and industry groups to lobby, the division of tasks means that no single committee or agency looks at environmental issues as a whole.

Question: What stands between us and energy independence?

Answer: A tangled web of government departments, agencies and committees — a small sampling of which you can see below:

Executive Branch:

Federal Agency	Environmental Responsibilities
White House Office	Overall policy, agency coordination
Office of Management and Budget	Budget, agency coordination and management
Council on Environmental Quality	Environmental policy, agency coordination, environmental impact statements
Department of Health and Human Services	Health
Environmental Protection Agency	Air and water pollution, solid waste, radiation, pesticides, noise, toxic substances
Department of Justice	Environmental litigation
Department of the Interior	Public lands, energy, minerals, national parks
Department of Agriculture	Forestry, soil, conservation
Department of Defense	Civil works construction, dredge and fill permits, pollution control from defense facilities
Nuclear Regulatory Commission	License and regulate nuclear power
Department of State	International environment
Department of Commerce	Oceanic and atmospheric monitoring and research
Department of Labor	Occupational health
Department of Housing and Urban Development	Housing, urban parks, urban planning
Department of Transportation	Mass transit, roads, aircraft noise, oil pollution

Department of Energy	Energy policy coordination, Petroleum allocation research and development
Tennessee Valley Authority	Electric power generation

Senate:

Committee on Agriculture, Nutrition and Forestry	Pesticides
Committee on Appropriations	Appropriations
Committee on the Budget	Budget
Committee on Commerce, Science, and Transportation	Oceans, research and development, radiation, toxins
Committee on Energy and Natural Resources	Synthetic fuels, conservation oversight, energy budget, mines, oil shale, outer continental shelf, strip mining
Committee on Environment and Public Works	Air, drinking water, noise, nuclear energy, ocean dumping, outer continental shelf, research and development, solid waste, toxins, water
Committee on Foreign Relations	International environment
Committee on Homeland Security and Governmental Affairs	Interagency subject area
Committee on Labor and Human Resources	Public health
Committee on Small Business	Impact of environmental regulations on small business

House:

Committee on Agriculture	Pesticides
Committee on Appropriations	Appropriations
Committee on the Budget	Budget
Committee on Oversight and Government Reform	Interagency subject area
Committee on Interior and Insular Affairs	Synthetic fuels, conservation oversight, energy budget, mines, oil shale, outer continental shelf, radiation (Nuclear Regulatory Commission oversight), strip mining
Committee on Energy and Commerce	Air, drinking water, noise, radiation, solid waste, Toxins
Committee on Natural Resources	Ocean dumping
Committee on Transportation and Infrastructure	Noise, water pollution, water resources
Committee on Science and Technology	Research and development
Committee on Small Business	Impact of environmental regulations on small business

Are all of these departments, committees and offices communicating in concert? Are they all congruent in their purposes, functions and responsibilities? No, they all have different responsibilities and self-serving agendas. But what about their values, missions and communication? They are non-existent.

The federal government provided substantially larger subsidies to fossil fuels than to renewables in the 2002–2008 period. Subsidies to fossil fuels totaled approximately $72 billion over the study period, representing a direct cost to taxpayers. Subsidies for renewable fuels totaled $29 billion over the same period.

Everyone—conservatives, liberals and the Common Sense 80%— agrees that renewable energy holds the only logical future for us, but we are subsidizing fossil fuels by a factor of more than 3:1, which furthers the argument for term limits and reducing the influence of lobbyists.

Solution: Drill for Both.

How do we balance environment, energy, conservation, foreign policy, trade and renewable fuels? Simple. The common sense in all of us dictates that:

1. **We agree that we need to reduce our dependency on foreign oil.** Importing oil helps fund countries and cultures that want to destroy the United States (or as they refer to us, the "Great Satan").

2. **We need to continue to lead in being the cleanest energy country.** As the leader in clean technology (a view of any Russian or Mexican oil field will support this), we are the most environmentally responsible oil-producing country on the planet. The logical extension is the more oil we develop, the cleaner the world will be. Let's put the dirty developers of oil out of business. Strictly from an environmental viewpoint, we should be encouraging the United States to develop more oil. The more we depend on "dirty" developers, the more we are encouraging environmental irresponsibility.

3. **We need to be developing aggressively new energy technologies that will allow us to shift our dependence on fossil fuels toward renewable energy**, even as we aggressively develop our own oil and wean ourselves from the teat of the very people who want to destroy us,. Most renewable sources are cleaner and become cheaper over time. The Common Sense 80% all agree that it is absolutely necessary to develop solar, wind, geothermal, biofuels and fuel cells.

The sooner we can eliminate the lobbying power, install term limits and allocate our research and development and influence to renewable energy, the more real national security we will have and the cleaner our world will become.

In the meantime, as the most responsible and cleanest driller on the planet, we should focus 100% of our current efforts on opening up all of our oil and reserves. Starve OPEC of its top customer and make our nation more secure.

Regarding the environment, let's take a long-term view. We can rightfully assume that even with advances in technology, which have previously doubled our oil supply, oil will eventually be depleted. It is not a renewable resource, and one day it will be depleted to the point where economies won't be using it.

The bottom line is we need to stop supporting terrorist regimes and wean ourselves from the teat of the overpriced oil they are selling us. Our national security is at risk with every gallon we purchase from the Middle East. We are the cleanest producer of oil, so, environmentally speaking, we need to encourage more development inside our borders (and outside our borders when we control or lease from other nations). As the environmental leader of the world, the more we do, the less "dirty" drilling, the less our national security becomes at risk.

Drill and develop oil at home, responsibly and abundantly. Develop renewable resources and celebrate innovation. It's our only shot at achieving true independence.

Conclusion

You Can't Legislate Stupidity

—◊◊—

There is a culture of disgust brewing in America. It doesn't matter if this angst is labeled the Tea Party or Occupy Wall Street. As a general rule, Americans are smart people, and we all know intuitively that our economy has massive potential and that our federal government is so big, bloated and corrupt that trimming it, reducing it or adjusting it is nearly impossible.

There are not many legislators who are also Kamikaze pilots, but they should be. They all know one hundred times more than you or me about the corruption, greed, scandal and the unreported, egregious waste that occurs in Washington. But, they all are too cowardly to do anything to upset the apple cart that pays for their re-election campaigns, just so they can keep on living the good life in D.C.

Too bad.

If even a minority of 10% or so would call a press conference, resign, throw in the towel and call out the remaining 90%, they would not only be lauded as American heroes, but they could be the catalyst for the radical change that is necessary to put America back on the road to abundance, respect and honor.

If we continue to complain without doing anything, we all lose. If we ignore the obvious and keep adding fuel to the fire to the extreme left or right of any issue, we all lose. The Common Sense 80% solution is one upon which almost all of us agree. Nobody in his or her right mind believes the federal government is the best solution for everything—or anything, for that matter.

When we don't balance our books, there is a consequence. When the government doesn't balance its books, they enslave us and our future generations with a debt that we can never repay. Maybe we won't suffer temporarily as they can always print more money. But, they are paving a clear path for the collapse of the greatest nation on Earth.

Our expenses have far outpaced our income for a long enough period of time. The United States is bankrupt and, at some point, someone in a leadership position is going to have to stop passing the blame and step up and admit it— then get out of the way so the rest of us can clean up after them.

The federal government is an emotionless, faceless machine that knows no consequences and feels no pain. When things go wrong, there are nearly 3,000,000 federal workers to blame. With a federal government this massive, accountability to finances and consequences of results make the leadership of a team impossible.

Our country, like so many civilizations before us that got fat and happy, is on a particular course of decline. With over $140,000,000,000,000 in debt and unfunded liabilities—and no courage to step up and fix it in Washington— our only hope is for a radical, logical, grassroots movement to take hold and force the issue.

We, the Common Sense 80%, are obligated to act. We can be a force for change.

It is not too late.

Our action is required.

Take ACTION
The Agreement

—⚏—

We've mentioned "The Agreement" throughout this book.

The Agreement is a simple document to be used by candidates running on the Common Sense 80% platform. Why include a document like this? Several reasons:

1) It explains exactly what you, as a candidate stands for.

2) It clearly states your plan of action once you are elected.

3) It allows a voter to vote for the Common Sense 80% platform candidate and, to a certain degree, takes the focus off the candidates' personality and places it VERY clearly on the platform. It brings the issues directly to the forefront of the discussion and leaves the "popularity contest" to trail.

4) Most importantly, included in The Agreement is a fully executed and notarized resignation by the candidate that is placed in escrow so that his/her constituents can dump the candidate immediately if he/she doesn't strictly follow their campaign promises. ZERO room for compromise. It is literally the only way we can turn this country around quickly. It is a full-on commitment by the candidate to put his/ her money where their mouth is. This is a contract for statesmen only, no career politicians. With The Agreement, their word is literally their bond.

The Agreement is an "etched in stone," unwavering promise by those who step up and run on the Common Sense 80% platform to do the right thing . . . to take decisive, responsible action and promise to follow through WITHOUT COMPROMISE. The Agreement will act as a straightforward and brief manual for leaders and supporters of the Common Sense 80% Revolution that is happening now.

When people start to run for office in the coming months and years, the more who state, unequivocally, that they are running on this platform, the better. This is a platform that 80% of the country knows in their heart is long overdue and we are now ready to fight for it aggressively. Many of the Common Sense 80% issues were clearly supported in the 2016 election, and the movement is gaining steam!

Our great country is more than simply awash with debt. We are on the verge of insolvency. It is poised for a complete failure in currency, economy and funding. Even worse, good solid American values and principles are fading—quickly!

As you finish reading this page, assuming it takes you about 60 seconds, the national debt will increase by approximately $3 million, and the choking and stifling business and personal regulations brought about by the collusion of government, big corporations and special interests continue to pile upon us with each tick of the clock.

Read that again.

The national debt increases $3 MILLION per minute. This spiral is beyond anything imaginable, and any amount of budget cutting is equivalent to a spit in the ocean. Cutting a few billion here or there over the course of a year, or ten years even, won't change the one-way express lane that America is on to disaster.

On this road, the destination is very clear. The United States, for all practical purposes, is fiscally and culturally bankrupt.

And we can stop it.

You may think that one person can't make much of a difference. If there were only one copy of this book or one entry on a blog or one voice shouting on Capitol Hill, you would be right. But that isn't the case. The establishment of political frauds on both sides of the aisle is being called out for what they are. They are not statesmen. They are there to serve big money corporate special interests that keep them in office.

Look at the 2016 election and several elections before. The establishment has never been more vulnerable, and it is our time to give them the boot once and for all so that we can clean up D.C. There's a new sheriff in town, and it is us—the good, hardworking American people. We no longer have to bite our tongue and hide behind political correctness. As a movement, we are MANY and growing. Washington is about to get the enema that it has long needed.

The Agreement is a clear and non-partisan method to radically take our country back to its core principles and purpose. We must return our country to the fundamental values and fiscal responsibility we once had not too many years ago and, at the same time, empower states and local governments to be able to operate without interference.

Military, Monetary, Postal and Judicial. That's it.

The Agreement is a simple document to follow, and I encourage you to share it whenever possible. If you run for office, run on this platform with The Agreement fully signed, notarized and in escrow. It is your GUARANTEE to your constituency that you WILL do the right thing. If you recruit, support and/or vote for someone, insist they run on and HONOR the Common Sense 80% platform.

The message may sound alarmist, but to those of us who are personally accountable for our own actions, the Common Sense 80% platform is already second nature to us. We take personal responsibility for our own actions and act with integrity. We are demanding that our government step up and do the same.

The time has come.

It is simply COMMON SENSE.

The Agreement

Date: _____

I, _____, a candidate for The United States _____
from the great state of _____, hereby promise and pledge
the following to my constituency:

I.   I fully recognize that our country is in dire need of swift, bold,
     immediate and non-compromising action that will return our
     country to the fiscally and culturally rich nation which was
     intended by our Founding Fathers as set out in the Constitution and
     the Bill of Rights.

II. I am willing to step up and lead the effort to join with other Common
     Sense Candidates to take such necessary actions, and I promise
     NEVER to compromise.

Wherefore:

1.   When running for office, I will only take donations from individuals
     and businesses who are based in my district (for Representatives)
     and state (for Senators). Under no circumstances will I take campaign
     contributions from anyone, business or PAC, who does not live in, is
     not based in, or does not directly represent my constituency.

2.   Immediately upon taking office, I promise to introduce and/or support
     legislation that limits political donations for U.S. House and Senate
     campaigns to come only from individuals or businesses based in their
     districts (for House seats) or state (for Senate seats).

3.   Immediately upon taking office, I promise to introduce and/or support
     legislation that puts a cap on campaign spending for U.S. House and

Senate seats that would limit campaign spending to an amount equal to $1.00 per resident in their constituency with increases in that amount tied to a cost of living index.

4. If elected, I promise to serve for a single term in office and not to run for re-election. Additionally, I promise to not accept a government appointment, government job or lobbyist position. I promise not to run for any other public office for a period of at least five years from the time I leave office.

5. Immediately upon taking office, I promise to introduce and/or support a law requiring term limits that limit the members of the United States House of Representatives and members of the United States Senate to ONE consecutive term only. Additionally, elected members must not accept a government appointment, government job or lobbyist position after the elected term is over. He/she is not to run for any other public office for a period of at least five years from the time the initial elected term has ended. This is out of recognition and acknowledgment that, under the current system, a member of Congress is forced to spend as much or more time on fundraising for their next election than they do fulfilling their duties as a legislator. A member of Congress can never truly vote their conscious and perform in the best interest of their constituency as long as they are having to raise money and be beholden to lobbyists, big corporations and special interest groups.

6. Immediately upon taking office, I promise to introduce and/or support legislation that requires the federal government to operate on a balanced budget that allows for surpluses to be accumulated.

7. Immediately upon taking office, I promise to introduce and/or support legislation that will eliminate and defund all non-essential departments from the federal government. These include government departments,

agencies and programs that do not fall under the tasks of Monetary, Military, Postal, Judicial or National Transportation completely, and to return the power to the states, allowing the states to form co-ops for services needed across the states.

8. I promise to only enact new legislation that puts into action government duties that cannot reasonably be carried out at the state or local level, either as individual states or by a co-op of the states.

9. Immediately upon taking office, I promise to introduce and/or support legislation that defunds all federal grants and subsidies.

10. Immediately upon taking office, I promise to introduce and/or support legislation that would begin maximizing and liquidating federal government assets so that the proceeds can be used to pay down debt and obligations owed to the taxpayers.

11. Immediately upon taking office, I promise to propose and/or support legislation that will replace the current individual income tax with a 10% national consumption tax (with no exceptions, deductions or exclusions) so that individual taxpayers never have to file a tax return again.

12. Immediately upon taking office, I promise to introduce and/or support legislation that would begin the process of the government: a) issuing I.O.U.s to the taxpayers who chose to exit the programs into which they have paid, and b) delivering the benefits, through a private sector service, for the people who choose to remain enrolled in the government program in which they have paid. I fully believe that Social Security, Medicare and other government financial schemes no longer efficiently serve the people of the United States. Furthermore, I believe that the government has wrongfully managed that money and that taxpayers are rightfully owed either: a) a refund

plus interest on the money and benefits that they have not yet withdrawn, or b) the full benefit of the service of the obligation they paid for.

13. Immediately upon taking office, I promise to introduce and/or support legislation that will strip the ability of government unions to operate.

14. I promise to promote and/or support only free market policies, and to aggressively roll back and abolish any current regulations and/or programs that do not fully support free market policies.

15. Immediately upon taking office, I promise to introduce and/or support legislation that would require that every bill be a single purpose bill that must stand alone on its own merit.

16. Immediately upon taking office, I promise to propose and/or support the Common Sense 80% immigration policy whereby an immigrant can apply for a ten-year temporary resident status under the following qualifications:

a) The petitioner and/or their dependents have ZERO criminal past.

b) The petitioner and/or their dependents have never EVER taken welfare and public assistance from any government entity in the United States—federal, state or local.

c) The petitioner agrees to never apply for or take welfare and/or accept public assistance of any kind from any government entity in the United States.

d) The petitioner and dependents are sponsored by two natural-born American citizens who, for a period of ten years, will stand good for and personally guarantee (with an actual financial guarantee) that the petitioning party and their dependents will not commit a crime, will not apply for or accept any public assistance from any government entity in the United States, including federal, state or local, and will stand good for all debts incurred and defaulted on by the petitioner. If the petitioner does apply for or accept any such public assistance, the guarantor will be held fully responsible for any and all money accepted and/or court costs incurred, fines or penalties levied upon the petitioner as a result of any crime they commit or debt in which they default.

e) Upon the completion of their ten-year temporary resident status and provided they have fulfilled all of the requirements of their immigration commitment, the petitioner can apply to become a full resident of the United States of America.

17. Immediately upon taking office, I promise to do a live interactive video call for my constituents every week, giving a status report on my past week's activity in office, the general activity of the chamber in which I serve, and to take constituent questions and requests on the call. Along with this, I promise to post online a complete detailed calendar of all meetings scheduled in my capacity as a member of Congress.

18. Immediately upon taking office, I promise that all meetings with lobbyists and corporate donors will be available for live broadcast as well as posted in permanent archives for public viewing. In my capacity as a member of Congress, I promise NEVER to meet with lobbyists, representatives of special interest groups, and/or corporate donors outside of an office where the meeting cannot be broadcast and recorded.

19. Immediately upon taking office, I promise to introduce and/or support legislation that would limit sessions (full sessions and committee hearings) in both houses of Congress to 60 days, and would require members of the House of Representatives and Senate to spend a minimum of 225 days outside of Washington D.C. in their districts (for Representatives) or states (for Senators).

20. Immediately upon taking office, I promise to introduce and/or support legislation that distributes the headquarters of the remaining federal departments, agencies and programs to locations around the United States and outside of the Washington, D.C. metro area. I believe that too much power is concentrated in Washington, D.C. Therefore, I promise to introduce and/or support legislation that would allow for Congressional sessions to be held in rotating locations around the country so that all citizens have the opportunity to observe and participate.

21. I promise to give any proposed action the Common Sense Litmus Test before I vote on it. If it doesn't pass the Common Sense Litmus Test (see below), I will vote against it.

The Common Sense Litmus Test:

A) Is the proposed action a function of the Military, Monetary, Postal, Federal Judiciary or National Transportation, and/or is it a function that cannot be managed on a state or local level? If yes, I will consider the action on its merits as a standalone issue. If not, I will fully oppose it.

B) Does the proposed action introduce a new regulation? If yes, unless it is a matter of national security, I will oppose it.

22. I hereby place into escrow my resignation that may be filed if I breach this agreement.

HEREBY AGREED ON THIS _____ DAY OF_____
, 20_____.

_____

Candidate

NOTARY

Escrow instructions attached.

Common Sense 80%—Epilogue

—∿—

B ut wait! Before we end, let's address the elephant in the room. (Well, actually, there are two elephants in the room, neither of which the establishment Republican or Democratic Party "leaders" like to acknowledge.) Let's start with the more obvious elephant. And it's a big one! Donald Trump.

Trump, a highly successful, controversial American businessman, recognized that our great country was on a fast track to disaster. Love him or hate him, he was at least willing to step up to the plate and put it all on the line. So he, along with a lot of other great Americans, had a shot at actually "making America great again." Knowing that his entire personal life would be turned upside down and shaken out for all the world to see, he still jumped into a fray of 16 Republican-establishment swamp candidates and beat them all. Badly! He literally risked it all to have the position and opportunity to take action and do something about trimming our bloated government, bringing a much needed attitude adjustment to the oppressive regulatory agencies stifling our economy, bringing respect back to our rapidly weakening standing on the world stage, and, most of all, being a champion of our nearly forgotten Constitution.

The establishment Republican swampers were, and continue to be, so out of touch with us—the American citizens—that they didn't see it coming. We—average Americans who love our country and appreciate the freedoms granted to us under the Constitution—understand those freedoms and we truly enjoy and act on our "right to the pursuit of happiness." And, perhaps most importantly, we had had all of the self-serving establishment swampers we could take.

One of my good friends, a right leaning comedian, joked that when Jeb Bush announced his candidacy, the campaign conducted a survey amongst the Republican base and the only name that polled worse than Bush was "Ass Cancer." As it played out, that probably wasn't far from the truth. Bush spent a record $125 million in the 2016 primary and didn't even make it to the top five candidates. Americans had had all of the "swamp" they could take. Yes, folks, had Donald Trump not stepped up with his bold approach to Making America Great Again, November 8, 2016, could very well have seen a tight presidential election between Hillary Clinton and "Ass Cancer." For sure, a tough choice at the ballot box!

Which brings us to the lesser-celebrated but, nonetheless, other elephant in the room. Bernie Sanders. He's a likeable guy with batshit crazy, totally unsustainable socialistic ideas. Sanders actually, and proudly, proclaimed, "I AM A SOCIALIST." He was essentially proposing to turn America into the next Venezuela. And many Democrats, who were also exhausted with Hillary, (their own establishment swamper), almost elected him! And, I'm guessing that had the DNC not meddled in the primary, Nutty Uncle Bernie would have gotten the Democratic nomination.

Whatever the case, the base for both parties had had all of the establishment they could take. It was time for a change. And change we got. We have a President who, in his own brash way, is keeping the promises he made. He wakes up every morning having to go head-to-head with almost the entire "news" media, the crazy lefties, and even the swampers from his own party. But, he is tough, he loves America, and he pushes ahead, knowing that he has an army of great Americans who have his back. And yes, like many Americans, I cringe when I read some of the President's tweets and I wished he hadn't been banging porn stars back in the day. He's a colorful character and all those rough edges are what make him who he is. And none of it, good or bad, can change the fact that Trump is one of the VERY few elected officials who will actually do anything it takes to make good on his promises.

And now, because Donald Trump boldly blazed the trail for us, it is time for us, YOU and I, to step up and take "Making America Great Again" to the next level. Are you ready? Let's go!

Made in the USA
Las Vegas, NV
05 September 2021

29623469R00127